Equal Employment Opportunity

This study looks closely at labor market determinants—those that are assumed to be crucial and those that are usually ignored. It explores in depth the factors that contribute to or retard the penetration and mobility of blacks and women in employment in metropolitan areas in two different parts of the country. The industries selected for study—health and electrical manufacturing—are significant for both of these groups and provide structural contrasts. The author notes an uneven correlation between the number of available jobs and access to employment opportunities for women and blacks. He also examines other factors—political culture and structure, racial attitudes in the community, and black political power—of crucial importance to these groups' finding employment.

Conservation of Human Resources Series: 16

EQUAL EMPLOYMENT OPPORTUNITY

A Comparative Micro-analysis of Boston and Houston

ROBERT C. SMITH

Foreword by Eli Ginzberg

LandMark Studies

Allanheld, Osmun   Publishers

ALLANHELD, OSMUN & CO. PUBLISHERS, INC.

Published in the United States of America in 1982
by Allanheld, Osmun & Co. Publishers, Inc.
(A Division of Littlefield, Adams & Company)
81 Adams Drive, Totowa, New Jersey 07512

Copyright 1982 by Conservation of Human Resources

Library of Congress Cataloging in Publication Data

Smith, Robert Charles, 1947-
    Equal employment opportunity

    (Conservation of human resources series; 16)
(LandMark studies)
    Includes index.
    1. Discrimination in employment—Massachusetts—
Boston. 2. Discrimination in employment—Texas—Houston.
I. Title. II. Series.
HD4903.5.U58S57   331.13'3'0974461   82-1764
ISBN 0-86598-072-1   AACR2

82 83 84 / 10 9 8 7 6 5 4 3 2 1

Printed in the United States of America

Contents

List of Tables

Tables

Foreword

In the early 1960s, Professor Dale Hiestand of the Conservation of Human Resources (CHR) broke new ground in exploring the relations between Economic Growth and Employment Opportunities for Minorities (Columbia, 1964). About a decade later Professor Stanley Friedlander, another member of the staff, undertook a detailed analysis of Unemployment in the Urban Core: An Analysis of 30 Cities with Policy Recommendations (Praeger, 1972) which introduced spatial considerations into the assessment of how well or poorly the unemployed, including an overrepresentation of minorities, were faring in different locations.

The Civil Rights Act of 1964 and the subsequent governmental and nongovernmental efforts to lower the barriers to employment for Blacks, Hispanics, and women pointed to the desirability of undertaking comparative micro analysis. To that end the Conservation of Human Resources Project developed a proposal that the U.S. Department of Labor funded for an assessment of the employment gains achieved in the 1960s and 1970s by minorities and women, in Boston and Houston with the focus on two large industries: electronics and health care.

The research plan pointed to the desirability of a cooperative undertaking between a labor market specialist, skilled in the use of data analysis and a social scientist with broad interests and competence in the problems of minorities and the ways in which the political-social environment constrains or supports their efforts to improve their position.

Professor Katherine Lewis of the Graduate School of Business, Columbia University, and Professor Robert Smith at the State University of New York, Purchase, and more recently on the faculty of Howard University, were added to the CHR staff for this project.

Regrettably, Professor Lewis left the Graduate School of Business and CHR after the project was well underway but long before the analysis had been completed. It was fortunate indeed that Professor Smith volunteered to assume sole responsibility for seeing the project through to completion.

Let me indicate briefly what I consider the highlights of this effort and their implications for future research and policy to be.

--No matter how much economists strive and succeed to develop macro models of the labor market, no such models will be able to illuminate the range of behavior characteristic of a complex, rapidly changing, advanced industrial economy such as the United States with its marked variations by area, by industry, and by group workers. To understand what is happening over time to affect the jobs and earnings of black men or white and black women in a large labor market in the North or the South requires that the inquiry be structured to capture the relevant variables.

--Economists assume that if they can capture the essential relationships in the market, they can afford to neglect other parameters. But this is a questionable assumption when it comes to assessing changes in the penetration of groups that were previously discriminated against, such as minorities and women. The political, cultural, and social climate of the circumstances in which members of disadvantaged groups live and work is a major determinant of the rate in which the opportunity structure is likely to be altered in favor of the previously excluded.

--Important as these non-economic factors may be in shaping and reshaping the local labor market, it would be a serious error to ignore or downplay the rate of growth of total employment in the area. Employers are much more likely to broaden their conventional sources of recruitment to include minorities and women when facing a rapid buildup of their work force.

--Since large organizations tend to hire at the bottom and promote from within even a decade is a relatively short period to assess the extent to which previously discriminated against groups are succeeding in advancing into middle level and particularly high level jobs. A decade is sufficiently long to provide evidence with respect to the former but not the latter.

--Comparisons over time are further complicated by the fact that no community, and particularly no fast growing community, relies primarily much less exclusively on local inhabitants to provide all of the new employees it requires. Mobility continues

to be a dominant characteristic of the American worker
and over the last two decades a great many have moved
from near and far into Houston in response to the
rapid expansion of the economy; and to a lesser degree
the same has been true for Boston.

--From the viewpoint of policy a sustained effort to
broaden opportunities for minorities and women may
require leadership by the federal government but it
clearly requires more participation by state and local
government and by leadership groups in the non-govern-
mental sector from employers to the spokesmen for
minorities and women. If the United States is a
pluralistic society - and it is - then it should be
clear that in such pervasive matters as reducing racism
and sexism only pluralistic efforts offer real prospects of success. Undue reliance on any single in-
strumentality is certain to prove disappointing.

--In the more mundane arena of employment and training
programs, clearly CETA in conception if not always in
execution was a move in the right direction by placing
primary responsibility on community leaders to design
intervention programs in light of the specific labor
market problems that required attention. While the
federal government could establish broad goals and
make funding available, the only prospect for improv-
ing the employability of the hard-to-employ was through
cooperation at the local level involving government,
business, education, labor and community based
organizations.

The present modest study of the employment changes of minorities and women in two industries in two cities undergoing
different rates of growth is nothing more, but also nothing
less than an exploratory effort. But I think it is fair to
conclude that it is an exploration that paid off by proving
that considerable insight could be gained by following such a
micro approach. We need more and if more are to yield deeper
insights we need better local labor market and community information.

Progress will not come easily but it will come if re-
searchers make the effort to build and improve on Professor
Smith's pioneering effort.

Eli Ginzberg, Director
Conservation of Human Resources
Columbia University

Acknowledgments

Professor Eli Ginzberg, founder and Director of the Conservation of Human Resources Project, initiated the study and provided assistance at every stage. Several of my colleagues at the Project also provided valuable assistance. Professors Charles Brecher, Dale Hiestand and Thomas Stanback read all or parts of the manuscript and made suggestions that led to improvements. Dr. Kathy Lewis and David Chunn processed the data, James Kuhn allowed me to consult his unpublished paper on the electrical manufacturing industry and Miriam Cukier served efficiently as expeditor and coordinator of the study through its varied phases. I should also like to thank Professor Alfred Eichner for his encouragement and assistance.

I am also indebted to the many officials at government agencies, labor unions, employer associations and other interest groups who provided information about the Houston and Boston labor markets and the health and electrical manufacturing industries. The Faculty Research Committee, Department of Political Science, Howard University provided support for typing the manuscript.

Like most of the work done at the Conservation of Human Resources Project, this study is in many ways a collaborative one. However, responsibility for errors of fact and analysis are exclusively my own.

CHAPTER 1
Introduction

Individuals seeking employment in the United States, except for certain professionals, managers and technicians, do not find work in a single, national labor market. Rather, they seek and find employment in particular local labor markets in the United States. That is, in general there is no national labor market but a series of interrelated local labor markets. The recognition of this fact is the point of departure of this study. This recognition stems from an awareness that national level, aggregate manpower studies, while valid and useful at that level, may conceal more than they reveal about the dynamics of local labor markets. Regarding employment policies, former Under Secretary of Labor Michael Moskow observed:

> It is important to realize in planning employment policy that the labor force is not monolithic; that there are major demographic, regional and industrial differences.... What is needed both at the technical and policy levels is a more thorough understanding, and a better knowledge of the adjustment process in potential bottleneck industries and labor markets.[1]

And regarding research on employment discrimination, Friedlander suggests,

> ...it is necessary to move beyond analysis of the national economy toward a disaggregated view of the operation of local urban labor markets. Despite the paucity of acceptable data, it is critical to examine these markets, for they are the focus of the major unemployment problems...

1

along with the government machinery to implement policies....[2]

In keeping with this emergent theme, the focus of this study is not at the national level. Instead, we study employment discrimination in the United States through a detailed examination of the workings of the economy in two metropolitan areas, Houston and Boston, and two industrial sectors, health care and electrical and electronics manufacturing, for the periods 1965-70 and 1970-75.

The two geographic labor markets were selected to represent areas with significant differences of social structure and political culture and because Boston represents a relatively slow growing economy and Houston a relatively rapid growing one. Our choice of Houston and Boston to represent respectively an ascending, rapid growth "sunbelt" city and a declining, slow growth "snowbelt" city has important implications for both research and policy. In terms of research, at the national level workers at the end of the queue generally do better in rapid growth economies than in slow growth ones. By focusing on these two local labor markets, we can more precisely delineate the impact of this factor on black and female employment. In terms of the impact on employment policy, this approach is potentially useful as a model in developing manpower policies that further the absorption process into regular and meaningful jobs for blacks and women throughout the United States.

The two industries were selected to represent a goods producing and a service producing sector and because the health industry has traditionally been a source of employment opportunities for blacks and women, while among the high wage manufacturing industries blacks and women have been traditionally underrepresented in electrical manufacturing. In addition, the health industry, because it was the target of important public policy initiatives in the 1960s, has experienced considerable growth in employment in recent years. The time span 1965-70 represents a period of important public policy changes with respect to equal employment opportunity as well as a period of rapid economic growth. The years 1970-75 were characterized by a general slow-down in the economy and a slow-down in the momentum of civil rights initiatives. Thus, the geographic locales, the industries and the time periods converge in the study to produce a tale of two cities that provides a special link between macro-economic policies and micro-level manpower considerations.

Design and Methodology

We seek to address specifically questions of the penetration and mobility of blacks and women in the two industries and

two locales. By penetration we mean the growing share of jobs
provided to women and black workers in each locale and sector.
Mobility is understood as the degree to which blacks and women
progress overtime through wage structures and job hierarchies.

Data on the work force characteristics of the industries
are drawn from the Social Security Administration's Continuous
Work History Sample (CWHS) for Houston and Boston for the
years 1965, 1970 and 1975.[3] This data base is used for several reasons. First, it is the only reasonably comprehensive
source of information about employee characteristics in specific localities and specific industries. Second, it is easily
partitioned into the race-sex categories that are of interest
to us: white males, black males, white females and black females. Third, it is a longitudinal data set. This permits
the more exact tracing of the extent of mobility in and out of
the industries. Fourth, it is a relatively large sample,
representing 1 percent of all workers in the Social Security
System. Thus we can have more confidence in the significance
and the reliability of the findings. The sample also provides
occupation-specific income distributions for individuals working in the industries. This data permits us to gauge the extent of mobility experienced by blacks and women in the industries by tracing progress through wage structures over time.

In addition to the data available from the Social Security
sample, supplementary information on the employment of blacks
and women in the two industries and cities was obtained from
the Equal Employment Opportunity Commission (EEOC). EEOC ad-
ministers Title VII of the Civil Rights Act of 1964 which
prohibits discrimination in employment on the basis of race,
color, religion, sex and national origin. EEOC is empowered
by Title VII to require such reports as are reasonable, necessary or appropriate for the enforcement of the Act. In this
connection, private employers have been required since 1966 to
file annual reports indicating the sex and racial/ethnic make-
up of their employees. The Commission's data on the employment of minorities (blacks, Hispanics, Asian-Americans and
American Indians) are reported by occupational categories for
the United States, the states, counties, and cities with populations of 50,000 or more. Thus it is a major source of
statistical information on the employment of blacks and women.
However, the reporting requirement under Title VII,[4] especially the exclusion of employers of less than 100 persons,
has a differential impact on coverage among industries, excluding firms or establishments characterized by small work
forces.[5] Thus for our purposes, the CWHS is a more basic and
comprehensive source of information. However, as a supplement
to the CWHS data the EEOC data for the periods 1966, 1970 and
1975 provide a useful cross-check. In addition, it permits us
to study more precisely mobility because the EEOC data report
employment by detailed occupational categories (officials and
managers, professionals, technicians, clerical, craft, opera-

tives, etc.) rather than simply by income as is the case with
the CWHS. Thus by comparing the two data sources, delineation
of the extent to which blacks and women have moved into higher
paying professional and technical jobs can be more precise.
Also, the differential between employment and mobility in the
two data sources allows us to make inferences about the impact
of Title VII on black and female access to employment opportunities.

Data on the social, economic and political characteristics
of the cities and the labor market characteristics of the industries are drawn from a variety of statistical sources including the 1970 Census of Population, Country Business Patterns, Census of Manufactures, Hospital Industry Wage Survey,
Standard Industrial Classification Manual, the Municipal Year-
book, etc. Additional material was obtained from correspond-
ence with a variety of institutions including the EEOC, the
Bureau of Labor Statistics, the Department of Health, Education and Welfare, the Office of Federal Contract Compliance,
the AFL-CIO and local interest groups and government authorities. Much of the statistical data on the cities is somewhat
dated. However, where available we have tried to provide more
recent information or indicate where possible the direction
and the extent of changes since the original data were col-
lected.

Explanatory Framework

Following Ray Marshall and his colleagues, we agree that
the "neoclassical" definition and formulation of the problem
of employment discrimination "have limited value . . . in understanding the employment disadvantages of blacks or pre-
scribing policies to eliminate it."[6]   Instead, they propose a
behavioral model "which looks at the behavioral characteristics
of employers, unions, government, interest groups, and individ-
duals in their interactions with each other and the environment
within which they operate."[7] Thus in this study we seek to explain black and female access to employment opportunities as a
function of four factors: Time, Place, Industry and Group.

Time as an explanatory factor is explored in the study
through analysis of differential employment and mobility of
blacks and women in the periods 1965-70 and 1970-75. These
time periods encompass important changes in the structure of
government and labor market behavior with respect to employment
opportunities for blacks and women. The years 1965-70 represent the period of the initial implementation of Title VII of
the Civil Rights Act of 1964 and the beginning of affirmative
efforts to employ previously excluded groups. The period also
represents a time of sustained economic growth nationally and
in these particular labor markets and industries. The period

of 1970-75 encompasses a recession and a period of relatively slow growth. Examination of these time periods thus facilitates inferential discussion of the impact of the equal opportunity laws and tight and slack labor markets on black and female employment opportunities.

Geographic place is, of course, basic to the study. Our central methodological assumption in the choice of Houston and Boston is that access by blacks and women to employment opportunities will vary between the two cities as a consequence of their differences in social, economic, political and labor market characteristics.

But individuals, as we said earlier, are not employed in Houston or Boston, rather they are employed in specific industries in Houston or Boston. Thus we examine the differential impact of industry characteristics on employment opportunities.

Finally, of course, we are interested in access by blacks and women to employment opportunities. Aside from time, place and industry, the access of such persons to employment is a function of characteristics of the group itself in terms of age, education, labor force participation, etc. Careful examination of these group characteristics also provides a means to make inferences about the contours of the group struggle (blacks vs whites, men vs women, black men vs white women) for employment and advancement in American industry.

This conceptual approach allows us to assess the relative weight of each of these factors on penetration and mobility among black and female workers. We believe this is a useful research strategy to identify in some detail distinctive features of particular industries in particular locales that play a part in the hiring and promotion of blacks and women.[8] In focusing on the employment and career mobility of black and female workers in this way we are searching for common and distinctive features underlying the labor market dynamics of particular industries and metropolitan areas with an eye toward considering these micro manpower dimensions in such a way as to construct sensitive and responsive national manpower policies. In addition, while our method and approach are narrow, we hope that they can serve as models for further work in the manpower and employment discrimination fields.

Outline of Chapters

In Chapter 2 basic descriptive information that distinguishes the two cities socially, economically, politically and culturally is presented. Chapter 3 presents data on the characteristics and structure of the two industries. In Chapters 4 and 5 the basic findings are presented and analyzed and in Chapter 6 the results are summarized and directions for research and policy are discussed.

NOTES

1. Remarks prepared for delivery at the 18th Annual Wilhelm
    Weinberg Labor-Management-Public Interest Seminar,
    Cornell University (November 14, 1970).
2. Stanley Friedlander, Unemployment in the Urban Core: An
    Analysis of Thirty Cities with Policy Recommendations
    (New York: Praeger, 1972), p. 5.
3. For discussion of the nature, availability, limitations
    and comparability of the data see Regional Work Force
    Characteristics and Migration Data: A Handbook on the
    Social Security Continuous Work History Sample and
    Its Application (Washington: U.S. Department of Commerce,
    Bureau of Economic Analysis, 1976).
4. Every private employer subject to Title VII and having
    one hundred or more employees was required in 1975 to
    file an EEO-1 report unless that employer was a primary
    or secondary school system, an institution of higher
    education, an Indian Tribe, or a tax exempt private mem-
    bership club other than a labor organization. Those
    federal contractors having fifty or more employees and
    contracts of at least $50,000 were also required to file
    in 1975. In 1975, a total of 35,500 employers filed re-
    ports covering 29.9 million workers. The EEOC estimates
    that these 29.9 million constitute forty-eight percent
    of all private, non-farm workers in the nation. Coverage
    among industries ranges from eighty-one percent in dura-
    ble goods manufacturing to fifteen percent in contract
    construction.
5. In 1975, according to calculations from County Business
    Patterns the average number of employees per reporting
    unit in the health care sector was 15.7 in Houston and
    18.7 in Boston. In the electronics and electrical manu-
    facturing industries the figures were 57.4 for Houston and
    91.6 for Boston.
6. Ray Marshall and Virgil Christain, "Economics of Employ-
    ment Discrimination" (Manuscript, 1974), p. 20.
7. Ibid., p. 21.
8. For an example of a study that explores the thesis that
    fundamental factors that shape employment patterns dif-
    fer significantly among major metropolitan areas and
    that these differences have a differential impact on
    the employment experiences and patterns of different
    groups in each metropolitan area see the recent study by
    Dale Hiestand and Dean Morse, Comparative Metropolitan
    Employment Complexes: New York, Chicago, Los Angeles,
    Houston and Atlanta (New York: Allanheld Osmun and Co.,
    1979).

CHAPTER 2
The Two Cities:
Social Structure and Labor Market

     We examine the workings of the labor market with respect
to employment discrimination in the Houston and Boston metropolitan areas.[1] In this chapter we present basic descriptive
information that distinguishes the two cities socially, economically, politically and culturally. These data are useful
for purposes of context and background and they provide a means
of explaining differences in the penetration and mobility of
blacks and women in the health and electrical manufacturing industries of the cities.

Social and Economic Structure

     In Table 2.1 data on basic social and economic character-
istics of the Houston and Boston Standard Metropolitan Statistical Areas (SMSAs) are presented. The most striking difference that emerges between the two areas is in terms of the relative proportions of their populations residing in the central
cities. As the table shows only 23 percent of the Boston
SMSA's population is in the boundaries of the city proper while
for Houston it is 62 percent, nearly three times the Boston
proportion. Boston's geographic boundaries are unusual. It is
a small seriously underbounded city surrounded by a number of
independent towns and cities. Because of these political boundaries, it is necessary to add the populations of surrounding
cities such as Cambridge and Somerville to get an accurate
sense of the size of the true "central city".[2]
     Houston is an extremely large city encompassing more than
500 square miles. In Houston, therefore, the political city
corresponds closely to the social city, while in Boston the
social city is highly fragmented politically.

TABLE 2.1

SELECTED SOCIAL AND ECONOMIC CHARACTERISTICS,

HOUSTON AND BOSTON STANDARD METROPOLITAN

STATISTICAL AREAS, 1970

Characteristic	Boston	Houston
Population	2,753,700	1,699,316
% population in Central City	23	62
% Black(a)	5.5	20
% Black in Central City	18.2	26.6
% Hispanic	1	17
% Hispanic in Central City	3	70
% Ethnic(b)	35.4	8.9
Median Age	29.1	25.8
% Population, 64 and Older	13	6
Sex Balance (Females for Males)	1.1	1.03
Median Income	$11,499	$10,191
% Income Above $15,000	30.1	22.6
% Income Below $3,000	6.1	9.8
Median Years of Education(c)	12.4	12.1
% High School Graduates	64.4	51.7
% College Graduates(d)	15.8	13.9

(a) Blacks and other races, Indians, Japanese, Chinese, Fili-
    pino. Blacks constitute about 92% of this category.
(b) Includes foreign born and native white population with
    foreign born or mixed parentage.
(c) Total persons, 25 years old and over.
(d) Total persons, 25 years old and over.

SOURCE: U.S. Bureau of the Census, Census of Population: 1970,
          Vol. 1, Characteristics of the Population, Part 23,
          Massachusetts; Part 45, Texas, Sections 1 and 2.

        This phenomenon of course is not unique to these particu-
lar cities. In general, cities of the south and southwest
(especially those in Texas) have been able to address the problems of urban sprawl with a policy tool unavailable to their
northern counterparts - the annexation of unincorporated
areas.[3] Consequently while the city of Boston expanded by
only three square miles between 1890 and 1970, Houston grew by
more than 300 square miles in the 20-year period of 1950-70.

     Similarly, Boston's population has been declining in re-
cent years while Houston has experienced phenomenal population
growth. From an all time high of 800,000 in 1950, the population of Boston has declined to an estimated 637,000 in 1979,
declining by 8.1 percent between 1960 and 1970. In Houston
between 1960 and 1970 the population increased by 31.2 percent
and in this decade the city's population has increased by 27.4
percent to an estimated 1,699,000.

     While the city of Boston has lost population, the SMSA
has continued to grow. Between 1960 and 1970 Boston's surrounding suburban communities grew by 6.1 percent. In Houston
the surrounding suburban communities in the period 1960-70
grew by 40 percent. In general, then, Boston conforms to the
emergent pattern of northeastern and mid-western cities, declining growth in the central city and population expansion in
the suburbs. Houston fits the pattern of the sunbelt: rapid
population growth in both city and suburb.

     In Boston the political fragmentation and the resulting
differential distribution of the populace between city and
suburb has resulted in many jobs being located outside the
central city where minority populations tend to be concentrated. As early as 1960 comparing Houston and Boston on the
spatial distribution of jobs, Friedlander found that 7.3 percent of the Houston SMSA's employment was in the suburban
ring. By 1966 this percentage had declined to a modest 6.7.
In Boston, however, fully 60.6 percent of the SMSA's employment
was in the suburban ring and by 1966 this had increased by 4.6
percent to 63.4 percent.[4] And specifically in the electronics
industry, Friedlander reports that "the route 128 complex of
electronics firms has grown enormously, increasing job dispersal
and a spatial barrier not easily bridged for residents of
Boston, particularly residents of the Roxbury slum."[5]

     This political fragmentation (and it should be clear that
it is a political rather than a labor market barrier that
leads to many jobs being located outside the city) also results
in fragmented, overlapping and inefficient delivery of government manpower, employment and equal opportunity services. For
example, in a recent research monograph for the Labor Department on the implementation of the CETA program in Boston and
eastern Massachusetts the authors report there is very little
cooperation between the Cambridge-Somerville program and that
of nearby Boston.[6]

     Both areas have substantial black populations. However,
they are distributed more widely over the metropolitan area
in Houston than in Boston. The black population of the Boston
SMSA is only 5.5 percent while for the city proper it is 18.2
percent. In Houston blacks constitute 26.6 percent of the
city's population but also 20 percent of the population of the
SMSA. Thus, again owing to the metropolitan fragmentation in
Boston as opposed to Houston, the black population is less

heavily concentrated in the central city in the latter than in the former.

We should be careful, however, in generalizing on the basis of these data since blacks in both cities tend to live in highly segregated communities on the fringes of the down-town area. In Boston, blacks occupy the South Bay and Roxbury areas south of the downtown area and a public housing project on Columbia Point. Similarly in Houston most blacks are con-centrated in a broad belt around Loop 610 downtown, running from southcentral Houston into the northcentral and north-eastern parts of the city. Thus even in Houston, to the ex-tent that job growth is taking place on the fringes of the city away from the downtown area, blacks face a potential spatial barrier to employment not unlike that in Boston.

The black population in both cities increased substan-tially in the last decade. From 1960 to 1970 the number of blacks in Boston increased from 63,276 to 104,707, up by 39.5 percent, and in Houston the black population increased by 31.8 percent, from 215,884 to 316,508. Since 1970 the black pro-portion of the population in Boston has increased, largely as a result of white out-migration and higher black birth rates rather than because of an influx of new black migrants. Precise figures will not be available until the 1980 census, but analysts at Boston's Redevelopment Authority estimate that between 1970 and 1976 the proportion of the city's black popu-lation increased from 17 to 21 percent (it is estimated that the city's overall population declined by about 1 percent during this period). In Houston, analysts at the City Plan-ning Commission estimate that the percent of the black popula-tion has remained roughly the same since 1970. The rapid growth in Houston's population during the 1970s is believed to include a mixture of rural southerners, black and white; upper-income blacks and whites from the North and Midwest; Mexican-Americans and foreigners (Mexicans and Arabs). Thus, blacks as a percentage of the city's population are believed to be in 1979 about what they were in 1970.

There is a major difference between the cities with re-spect to the size of the Hispanic population, the second largest and fastest growing minority group in the United States. The Hispanic population in Boston is relatively small, constituting 1 percent of the SMSA (3 percent of the city in 1970), and between 1970 and 1979 it is estimated that it has increased to 3 percent in the city. About half are Puerto Ricans who arrived in the 1960s and the remainder are Cuban and Central and South Americans. In Houston, the Hispanic popula-tion is primarily Mexican-American and constitutes 17 percent of the metropolitan area's population. Most are native-born Texans. Of the 212,000 Spanish language persons in the area, only 65,000 are foreign born or have a Mexican-born parent.

Boston has a higher percentage of persons of foreign stock than any large city except New York while Houston, as is typical of most southern cities, is overwhelmingly of native stock, although, as we indicated earlier, there has probably been some increase in Houston's foreign-born population in recent years. In 1970, 35.4 percent of Boston SMSA's population was foreign-born or native-born with foreign or mixed parentage. In Houston the comparable figure was 8.9 percent. Boston's large "ethnic" population is to a considerable degree segregated, with the Irish, Italians, Jews and "Yankees" residing in relatively distinct residential enclaves.[7] This "ethnic" diversity has been a persistent source of conflict and competition for jobs and housing.

In terms of more general social and economic characteristics, the two areas are basically comparable although Boston is slightly better off on gross measures of socio-economic well-being. As Table 2.1 shows, there is less poverty in Boston, the residents are better educated and have larger incomes. The elderly population is larger in Boston than in Houston, 11 percent and 6 percent of the SMSAs respectively. And in Boston there is a large student population in both city and suburbs. Houston has a more nearly equal sex balance, 1.03 females for each male while in Boston it is 1.1. In general, with the exception of the black population, in Houston there is little statistical difference between the city and surrounding suburban areas while in Boston the surrounding suburbs are somewhat better off on most measures of social and economic well-being.

Political Culture

Boston has often been viewed as the quintessential liberal city while Houston's civic culture has been described as one of pervasive conservatism. While to some extent both portraits are probably exaggerated, there is evidence to suggest that Boston is a more liberal city than Houston, using attitudes about the proper role and scope of government as the measure of liberalism-conservatism.

For example, in contrast to complaints about too much government in a city like Boston, critics in Houston argue that the city has too little government and that many voters prefer it that way.[8] Its lack of planning and zoning, its low taxes, its restrictive welfare policies and its commitment to uncontrolled growth are often cited as indicators of its conservative, anti-statist political culture. Size of the public sector is a good measure of political culture. Using data on the number of government employees as the measure, Houston with 11.3 employees per 1,000 and Boston with 25.8, Boston is clearly a much more conservative city. This is espe-

cially striking given the enormous size of the city of
Houston compared to Boston.

Using more traditional measures of liberalism, a similar
picture emerges. For example, calculation of the mean liberalism score of the cities' congressional delegations shows
that Boston's delegation has a mean score of 84 percent while
Houston's is only 47 percent.[9] To take another measure, Bos-
tonians supported George McGovern's liberal campaign of 1972
with 55 percent of their vote while the citizens of Houston
gave him only 32 percent.[10]

Houston's civic culture, then, compared to Boston's is
more likely to be hostile to minority employment opportunities to the extent that such opportunities are dependent on an
activist role by government since Houston is fairly described
as a city whose civic culture is premised on "the values of
privatism, individualism, religious fundamentalism, fiscal
conservatism, laissez-faire and a view of good government as
good business."[11] It should also be noted that "some of the
reasons for Houston city residents' distaste for active government are related to both class and race. Prosperous white
neighborhoods hire private security guards, garbage pickup
service and even private gardeners to tend city property in
their neighborhoods. They may spend as much on the services
as residents of other cities, but the money does not go
through the city government."[12] In sum, the political cultures of Houston and Boston differ in important respects and
these differences may affect minority access to employment
opportunities.

Political Structure and Minority Political Power

Until recently, the political structure in both cities
was characterized by the mayor-council form of government and
at-large, nonpartisan elections. At-large elections operate
to dissipate and dilute the potential political power of racial minorities in municipal elections[13] and most political
scientists agree that nonpartisan elections also tend to dilute the power of low-income, minority populations because
they remove the party label as a voting cue.[14] A referendum
on the ballot that would have created council and school committee districts for the first time in decades was defeated
in Boston in the most recent election, but in Houston recent
annexations came under review by the Justice Department to
determine whether the city diluted the voting strength of
minority groups by annexing six areas that were predominantly
white. Under Section V of the Voting Rights Act, Texas is one
of several states where any change that affects voting must
be reviewed by the Justice Department or the U.S. District
Court at Washington. As a result of the review, the Justice

Department required the city to institute a ward system under which the city would be divided into a number of districts that would each elect one member of the council. As a result, the new nine-member city council elected in 1980 has three blacks, two more than ever before.

Thus, in Houston black political power, measured by proportion of elective offices held in relationship to population is now significant. With a black population of 26.6 percent, blacks hold 24 percent of city offices including the three members of the council and two members of the ten-person school board. In Boston the black population is 18.2 percent, but blacks hold only 7 percent of city offices; none serve on the nine-member city council and it was only last year that a black was elected to the School Committee, the first in 75 years.[15] Indeed, this was only the second black elected to a city office in Boston in this century.

To the extent minority employment opportunities are related to the development of minority political power, as some scholars suggest,[16] then black access to employment opportunities in both cities, until recently, was weakened by the relative absence of political power. However, measured by percent of the black population (21 and older) who are members of the NAACP, black interest group power is greater in Boston than it is in Houston. The percentages, based on data provided by the NAACP national office, are 3 percent for Houston and 8 percent for Boston.

Similarly women in Houston constitute 19 percent of elected city officials including one member of the School Board, two members of the City Council and the City Controller, the latter elected in 1977 as the City's first female city official. In Boston, one woman serves on the nine-member Council and one on the five-person School Committee. Thus, in neither city have women, more than half the population, developed substantial political power, although more progress is evident in Houston than in Boston.

Race and Sex Attitudes

While we pay attention to those variables traditionally used in the analysis of minority access to employment opportunities, we also consider what are usually viewed as non-labor market variables. As Hiestand, among others, indicates, such variables, especially social change such as a decrease in racial prejudice and discrimination, may in the final analysis, be the primary determinant of minority employment and mobility.[17] Thus in this section we present indicators of racial and sex attitudes in the two cities. We begin with an analysis of housing and school segregation as proxy measures of racial attitudes.

As is the case in all metropolitan areas of the United States, there is racial segregation in housing and education. Table 2.2 presents information on the degree of racial isolation in the two school systems in 1970 and 1976. As the table shows there is substantially more segregation in Houston schools than in Boston. Both systems have come under court order to desegregate, however, as the data clearly show the far-reaching school desegregation process in Boston involving cross-city busing has been far more successful in ending racial isolation in the schools than the more limited magnet school program implemented in Houston. Although Massachusetts was the first state to enact a school desegregation law - the Racial Imbalance Act of 1965 - Boston schools were not desegregated until 1974. As a result of a Federal District Court order issued in June 1974, Phase I of the Boston process desegregated 80 of the city's 200 schools in September 1974. The following year, Phase II involved most of the remaining schools. Both phases involved cross-city busing of black and white children. Houston came under court order to desegregate its schools in 1970. A limited plan implemented that year paired 22 schools and involved only 20,000 of the more than 200,000 students in the district. In February 1975, a local Task Force for Quality Integrated Education recommended depairing of the schools. The board gained court approval for this action, and in the school years 1975-76 and 1976-77, 42 magnet schools enrolled approximately 25,000 students in this limited desegregation process.

TABLE 2.2

RACIAL ISOLATION IN THE HOUSTON AND BOSTON SCHOOL SYSTEMS,

1970, 1976

	Houston	Boston
% Blacks Attending Schools 90-100 % Black, 1970	73.7%	52.8%
% Blacks Attending Schools 90-100 % Black, 1976	63%	4%

SOURCE: U.S. Department of Health, Education and Welfare, Office of Civil Rights, Survey of Racial Isolation in the 100 Largest School Districts.

Thus, to the extent that degree of racial segregation in the schools is an indicator of racial attitudes, Boston is more racially accommodating than Houston. However, given the character and extent of the opposition to the desegrega- tion process in Boston, this finding requires at a minimum further support.

Such support is provided by Sorensen and his colleagues in their study of metropolitan housing segregation.[18] They report for 1970 a housing segregation index of 92.7 for Hous- ton and 84.3 for Boston (the index varies from 0-100, with 100 equaling complete segregation) indicating that Houston's housing, like its schools, is somewhat more segregated than is Boston's. This provides some further support for the prop- osition that Boston's racial attitudes are relatively more progressive.

Further support is developed by Friedlander in his 1972 study of 30 metropolitan labor markets including Houston and Boston.[19] Friedlander developed two measures of discrim- ination. The first, a crude measure of occupational discrim- ination based on the prevalence of nonwhites in low-status, low wage occupations, shows that occupational discrimination was far greater in Houston than in Boston and between 1960 and 1966 measured discrimination increased more in the former than in the latter. The data are reported below in Table 2.3.

TABLE 2.3

INDEX OF OCCUPATIONAL DISCRIMINATION*

	1960	1966	% Change
Houston	2.54	3.61	42.1
Boston	1.44	1.67	16

*An index of 1.00 would indicate that the percent of non- whites in each occupation is equivalent to whites.

SOURCE: Adapted from Stanley L. Friedlander, Unemployment in the Urban Core: An Analysis of Thirty Cities with Policy Recommendations (New York: Praeger, 1972).

In a more direct measure of racial discrimination, Friedlander developed an occupational-distribution index, ad- justed for relative educational attainment of whites and non- whites. This data, reported in Table 2.4, also show greater occupational discrimination in Houston than in Boston as well as a greater percentage growth.

TABLE 2.4

OCCUPATION - DISTRIBUTION INDEX ADJUSTED FOR RELATIVE

EDUCATIONAL ATTAINMENT OF WHITES AND NONWHITES*

	1960	1966	% Change
Houston	1.27	2.48	95.3
Boston	0.36	0.46	27.8

*A score that approaches zero reflects an absence of dis-
crimination.

SOURCE: Adapted from Stanley L. Friedlander, Unemployment in
          the Urban Core: An Analysis of Thirty Cities with
          Policy Recommendations (New York: Praeger, 1972).

It appears, then, that racial attitudes in Boston are more conducive to minority employment opportunities than those in Houston to the extent that such attitudes are related to employment opportunities. Or, to put it simply, while race and intergroup relations appear hostile, in Boston, the evidence points to the conclusion that there is relatively less prejudice and discrimination in Boston than in Houston.

The case of women is different.   They do not form hereditary social, economic and political communities, historically poor and oppressed. Rather, they are denied opportunities on the basis of traditional definitions of sex role.[20] One would expect, given that the South is the most traditional part of the country, given Houston's conservative civic culture and its fundamentalist religion, that the traditional role of women would be more pronounced in the attitudes of that city than in the relatively more liberal, cosmopolitan Boston. For example, the southern states have disproportionately failed to ratify the Equal Rights Amendment. And Pomper reports women now participate in voting at a rate equivalent to that found for men except in the South where regional culture still suppresses female participation.[21] This is evidence of a more traditional definition of sex roles that is likely to be present in southern cities such as Houston.

        We developed two measures to tap sex attitudes in the two
cities: percentage of women in professional occupations and
the percentage of women in traditionally male occupations, in
this case the police and fire forces. Neither of these two
measures distinguish the cities. Thirty-five percent of the
professional labor force in Houston and 39 percent in Boston
are female;[22] 3 percent of Boston's police are women and 6 percent of Houston's, and the Houston Fire Department employs one
woman, Boston none. (The participation of blacks and women in
the occupational structures of the cities is discussed in more
detail below.)
        Thus, while there is reason to believe that Houston's sex
attitudes are more traditional than Boston's, the evidence we
developed does not show this in terms of employment opportunities.

Labor Market: Growth and Decline

        Perhaps the most basic difference between the two labor
markets is in terms of employment growth; in Boston between
1960 and 1974 it is estimated at 19 percent, Houston at 106
percent. And 1979 unemployment figures show Houston with a
rate of 3.1, Boston 5.0. Thus these two labor markets offer
excellent cases for the study of the differential impact of
economic growth and tight labor markets on minority employment
and mobility.
        The employment growth figure for Boston understates the
dimensions of Boston's labor market problems. While there has
been growth in recent years, between 1950 and 1970, heavy job
losses occurred in Boston's manufacturing, transportation and
trade sectors. Gains were made in finance, services and
government but they were sufficient to raise the city's total
employment by only 2 percent over the 20-year period.[23]
Houston's economy during this period was experiencing phenomenal growth in all sectors, especially in chemicals, machinery
manufacturing, petroleum, energy technology, medical services
and the construction industry. The energy crisis of the last
several years has given added impetus to the growth of the
Houston economy. As a result between 1975 and March 1979 manufacturing employment was up by 20.5 percent in Houston but by
only 7.9 percent in Boston.
        The occupational structure of the two metropolitan areas
does not mirror these differences. Table 2.5 presents data on
the occupational structures of the SMSAs. It shows some differences between the two areas in terms of percentage white-
collar, government and manufacturing jobs. Boston has slightly more white-collar employment and Houston has a somewhat
larger number of persons employed by government at all levels,
state, local and federal. Nevertheless, for purposes of our

discussion in this chapter, the most basic point is that we
are dealing with radically different labor markets in terms
of the growth of employment opportunities in the last 20
years.

TABLE 2.5

OCCUPATIONAL STRUCTURE, HOUSTON AND BOSTON

SMSAs, 1970

	Houston	Boston
White Collar*	47.7%	59.6%
Manufacturing	20.2%	22.4%
Government	19.9%	15.6%

*Percent of total persons employed.

SOURCE: U.S. Bureau of the Census, Census of the Population:
1970, Vol. 1, Characteristics of the Population, Part
23, Massachusetts; Part 45, Texas, Sections 1 and 2.

Ethno-Sex Characteristics of the Labor Force

When examined in terms of age, education and distribution
in the professions and other high-paying occupations, several
differences emerge to distinguish the ethno-sex groups in the
two cities.

In Table 2.6 data are presented showing the age and educational levels of males, females and black males and females
in Boston and Houston. In both cities both black males and
females are somewhat younger than their white counterparts and
they possess somewhat less education, measured in terms of
median years and percentage of high school graduates.

Data on educational achievements of high school graduates
or seniors are not available by race or sex from the local
school authorities. We believe, in the absence of such data,
that the two cities in general conform to the national patterns. That is, we expect blacks and females to fall below
the national median on the various measures of educational attainment. Material available from the National Assessment of
Educational Progress shows that blacks fall substantially
below the median, 15.9 in science, 18.9 in writing, 18.7 in

TABLE 2.6

AGE AND EDUCATIONAL LEVELS MALES AND FEMALES BY

RACE IN HOUSTON AND BOSTON

	Houston	Boston
Median Age		
White Males	26.3	27.8
White Females	27.0	31.6
Black Males	21.6	20.6
Black Females*	22.9	23.3
Median Years of Education		
Males	12.1	12.4
Females	12.0	12.4
Black Males	10.0	11.6
Black Females	10.6	11.7
Percent Black Male High School Graduate	32.2	46.8
Percent Black Female High School Graduate	35.9	47.3

*Persons 25 years and over, data are for the SMSAs.

SOURCE: U.S. Bureau of the Census, Census of Population: 1970, Texas and Massachusetts.

reading and 24.5 in mathematics. Females are 4.7 below the median in science, 2.1 in writing, 0.3 below in reading and 5.0 below in mathematics.[24] These data suggest that the black and female labor force in general will not be as "qualified" as the white male labor force. Consequently, employers probably find the white male applicant pool marginally more desirable in terms of standard educational criteria than the pool of black and white female applicants.

Table 2.7 presents data on the percent distribution of women, black men and black women in professional, managerial and skilled craft positions. We indicated earlier that the percentage of women in professional positions is roughly comparable in both cities. As the table shows, there is similar

comparability in managerial and skilled craft positions with
women slightly better represented in the former in Houston
and the latter in Boston. These data show that women have
achieved reasonable representation in the professions and kindred occupations (given their participation in the labor
force), modest penetration in the managerial and administrative sectors and only the beginnings of representation in the
skilled crafts.

   Blacks in the two cities present a different pattern.
In neither of the cities have black males or females achieved
reasonable representation (in terms of percentage of population and labor force participation) in the professional, managerial or skilled craft sectors. Table 2.7 indicates, however, that blacks have made more progress in penetrating these
relatively privileged occupations in Boston than in Houston
(black men constitute approximately 2% of the labor force in
Boston and 10% in Houston; black women 1.9% in Boston and 8%

TABLE 2.7

ETHNO-SEXUAL DISTRIBUTION OF LABOR FORCE IN SELECTED

OCCUPATIONS, HOUSTON AND BOSTON, 1970

	Professional[a]	Managerial[b]	Craftsman
BOSTON			
Females	39%[c]	15%	4.6%
Black Males	1.1%	1.1%	2.9%
Black Females	1%	.3%	.1%
HOUSTON			
	Professional	Managerial	Craftsman
Females	35%	16.6%	3.8%
Black Males	2.9%	3%	11%
Black Females	5.5%	1.6%	.7%

[a]Professional, Technical and Kindred.
[b]Managerial and Administrative.
[c]Percentages are of total persons employed.

SOURCE: U.S. Bureau of the Census, Census of Population,
         1970, Texas and Massachusetts.

in Houston). This is especially the case for women in the
professions (5.5% Houston, 1% Boston) and for black men in the
managerial category (3% Houston, 1.1% Boston). This suggests
that the Boston labor market may have a more equal opportunity
structure in employment than Houston with respect to blacks.
In Table 2.8 more recent and detailed data on the participation of blacks and women in the occupational structures of
private industry in the two cities are presented. These data
show that in both cities women continue to be concentrated in
the relatively low-paying office/clerical and service categories. In Boston, twice as many women work as laborers and
there is somewhat more participation in the professions and
skilled crafts in Boston than Houston.

Black workers in both cities are concentrated in the low-
paying laborer and service categories with very little participation in the professional and managerial parts of the occupational structure of private industry. Comparing the EEOC
data in Table 2.8 with the census data in Table 2.7 one can
make inferences about the impact of Title VII on black and
female employment opportunities between 1970 and 1975. The
EEOC data are limited to private employers of a certain size
while the census covers the entire labor force. For the period 1970-75, the data suggest that the impact of EEOC's enforcement of Title VII has been minimal.

For example, in 1970 women constituted 39 percent of the
professional work force in Boston, 35 percent in Houston. In
1975, women constituted 31.8 percent of the professionals in
private industry in Boston and 21.8 percent in Houston. We
infer from these differences that Title VII enforcement has
not had a major impact on female access to employment opportunities in either city and that women are more likely to find
opportunities for advancement in firms not covered by EEOC,
that is in government or small business, probably in the former.

Similarly with blacks, the 1970 census showed 1.1 percent
black males in the professions in Boston, 2.9 percent in
Houston. The 1975 EEOC data show 1.3 percent black males in
the professions in Boston and 2.1 percent in Houston. This
again suggests minimal impact of EEOC and more opportunities
in the public sector than the private. In the cases of women
in both cities and blacks in Houston the percentage of persons
in the professions declines between 1970 and 1975. And while
this decline is probably a function of the more restrictive
coverage of EEOC data, it nevertheless argues for less than an
effective equal opportunity policy in both cities.

With respect to more employment opportunities in the public sector than in private industry, blacks have always found
more and better employment opportunities in the public sector
than in the private. For example, Brimmer reports that in 1974
public sector employment accounted for 21.6 percent of the
total number of jobs held by blacks but only 16.1 percent of
the proportion for all workers. Public sector employment

TABLE 2.8

ETHNO-SEX PARTICIPATION IN SELECTED OCCUPATION IN PRIVATE INDUSTRY, HOUSTON AND BOSTON, 1975

BOSTON

	Officials & Managers	Professionals	Office & Clerical Workers	Craft-workers	Laborers	Service Workers
Females	15.8	31.8	81.1	6.9	38.8	52.8
Black Males	1.3	1.3	1.1	3.5	5.5	6.5
Black Females	.6	.9	4.8	.4	4.1	6.6

HOUSTON

	Officials & Managers	Professionals	Office & Clerical Workers	Craft-workers	Laborers	Service Workers
Females	11.8	21.1	81.4	3.6	16.2	54.0
Black Males	2.9	2.1	2.5	12.1	31.0	15.0
Black Females	1.1	2.1	10.4	.7	6.3	23.4

SOURCE: Equal Employment Opportunity Report: Job Patterns for Minorities and Women in Private Industry, 1975 Vol. 2 (Washington: Government Printing Office, 1977).

also tends to pay much better than jobs held by blacks in the private sector, on average about 26 percent more.[26]

Labor Force Participation, Unemployment, Subemployment and Welfare

Labor force participation rates by ethno-sex characteristics vary in the two cities. The data reported in Table 2.9 show that adult males participate more in Houston, adult females more in Boston and that young people, male and female, participate more in Boston. In both cities adult males participate at a rate substantially higher than women. Young males also participate more than young females although the differences are not nearly as great as they are in the adult category.

TABLE 2.9

LABOR FORCE PARTICIPATION BY RACE, SEX AND AGE,

HOUSTON AND BOSTON, 1970

	Houston	Boston
Males, 16 years and over	82.2%	77.7%
Females, 16 years and over	43.6%	45.3%
Males, 16-19	47.7%	50.7%
Females, 16-19	31.6%	45.3%
Negro Males, 16 years and over	74.4%	72.1%
Negro Females, 16 years and over	52.3%	47.9%
Negro Males, 16-19	38.9%	40.0%
Negro Females, 16-19	25.7%	37.9%

SOURCE: U.S. Bureau of the Census, Census of Population: 1970, Texas and Massachusetts.

Black adults participate more in Houston, black youth in Boston. And in both cities the black female participation rate is somewhat greater than the white female rate. Overall, in both cities black labor force participation is less than that of whites.

Turning to the other face of labor force participation, the unemployment rate in 1970 was officially reported at 3.5 percent for the Boston SMSA (4.3 percent in the city) and 3 percent for the Houston SMSA (3.1 percent in the city). However, we know that this official rate understates the degree of joblessness by failing to consider the discouraged worker. We also know that an unemployment rate adjusted for the discouraged worker understates the failure adequately to employ human resources because it fails to take account of persons involuntarily employed part-time and those employed at substandard wages. These problems are especially acute in the case of inner city minorities.

Taking account of these deficiencies in the standard measure of unemployment, David Perry and Alfred Watkins in a recent paper develop indices that more fully measure the degree of unemployment and subemployment in nine "sunbelt" inner cities and a comparable number of "snowbelt" inner cities, including Houston and Boston. Their findings for Houston and Boston are adapted below in Table 2.10.

Perry and Watkins show that in 1970 the unemployment rate (counting the discouraged worker) in the Boston inner city was 26.8 percent and in Houston substantially less at 10.5 percent. In Houston 3.7 percent were involuntarily employed part-time, Boston 1.6 percent and 27.9 percent were working at substandard wages in Boston (using the Bureau of Labor Statistics' definition of a substandard wage), 45.3 percent in Houston. Overall, putting the unemployment and subemployment rates together, the figures for Houston and Boston are 59.5 percent and 55.7 percent respectively for primary wage earners in inner city families.

These data clearly demonstrate the enormous underutilization of human resources among inner-city residents of Houston and Boston. The Boston labor market simply fails to employ large numbers of inner-city residents and Houston's employs them, but at inadequate wages. Perry and Watkins summarize the import of their analysis of these data:

> ...A worker in a sunbelt city is more than twice
> as likely to be working full-time and receiving
> wages which are insufficient to provide a level
> of income above the poverty level.... In the
> northeast, however, the incidence of joblessness
> is greater but for those individuals or family
> heads who are working, the market has provided them
> with a larger share of good jobs.... Thus poverty
> in the sunbelt is in large part the result of low
> paying jobs.... While people living in poverty in
> the north are more likely to be unemployed
> because there is no job, or because they cannot
> find a job which meets their qualitative needs.[26]

TABLE 2.10

COMPARISON OF INNER-CITY SUBEMPLOYMENT RATES FOR THE PRIMARY WAGE EARNER

IN HOUSTON AND BOSTON, 1970 (in percentages)

Cities	UNEMPLOYED		Sub-total (1+2)	UNDEREMPLOYED	Full Time Workers $0.00 $2.00 $2.00 $3.50	Subtotal (4+5+6)	TOTAL (3+7)
	Unemployed	Discourages Workers		Involun tary Part Time Workers			
Boston	5.0	21.8	26.8	1.6	4.6 22.7	28.9	55.7
Houston	2.5	8.0	10.5	3.7	13.0 32.2	49.0	59.5

SOURCE: Adapted from David C. Perry and Alfred J. Watkins, "People, Profit and the Rise of the Sunbelt Cities," in Perry and Watkins, eds., The Rise of the Sunbelt Cities (Beverley Hills: Sage, 1977): 296.

25

Related to this distinct "sunbelt-snowbelt" pattern of employment, joblessness and poverty is, of course, the problem of welfare. The relationship between work and welfare in the United States is unclear. The findings from the large-scale, government-sponsored income maintenance experiments illustrate the ambiguity. The New Jersey experiment found no apparent relationship between the willingness of persons to work and the receipt of a guaranteed income while the results of a similar experiment in Seattle appear to show the opposite.

It is unclear whether these conflicting findings are the result of differences in design and execution or of differences between Seattle and southern New Jersey. But in any study of employment, especially minority access to employment one must consider the structure and operation of the welfare system as an adjunct to the labor market.

There are clear differences in the welfare systems of Houston and Boston. In 1966, Friedlander reported welfare cases per 1,000 population in Houston at 1.1, about the same as the 1960 level of 1.2. In Boston, welfare case per 1,000 in 1960 was 6.4 and by 1966 had increased by 131.3 percent to 14.8 per 1000. The payment levels also differed. In Boston payments per recipient per month in 1966 were $53.48 while in Houston they were $20.85.[27] By 1979, welfare cases per 1000 had increased to 41.4 in Boston, but to only 8.1 in Houston and the payment levels remained disparate, $95.62 per recipient per month in Boston, $32.40 in Houston. Of the nation's largest cities, Houston and the other major cities of Texas have the lowest welfare levels, Boston among the highest.

In Table 2.11, information on persons receiving public assistance as a source of income is presented by race, female-headed household and poverty status for Houston and Boston in 1970. In every category - female-headed families, families below poverty level, female-headed families below poverty level, black families below poverty level and black female-headed families below poverty level - Boston provides much more assistance than does Houston.

Thus, as an alternative to employment as a source of income and livelihood, individuals and families in Boston may and often do seek public assistance. In Houston this is more difficult, the criteria are more restrictive and the payment levels less adequate. Thus, some citizens in Houston are in a sense "forced" to work, whatever the wage, in order to support themselves and their families. As Perry and Watkins succinctly put it, "Sunbelt poverty is maintained and managed by the private sector, while northeastern poverty, now economically unmaintainable, is becoming increasingly the management problem of the state. What is a 'cheap labor' supply in the South, is a source of rising 'fiscal crisis' in the Northeast."[28]

Thus a more generous system in Boston in terms of payment levels and acceptance rates permits workers to use welfare as

TABLE 2.11

FAMILIES RECEIVING PUBLIC ASSISTANCE AS A SOURCE OF INCOME BY

RACE, HEAD OF HOUSEHOLD AND POVERTY STATUS, HOUSTON

AND BOSTON, 1970

	Houston	Boston
All Families	0.3%	6.5%
All Families, Female Heads	2.1%	24.6%
Families Below Poverty Level	5.7%	30.8%
Families Below Poverty Level, Female Heads	12.4%	51.2%
Black Families	9.0%	28.4%
Black Families, Female Heads	22.6%	56.9%
Black Families Below Poverty Level	18.8%	58.7%
Black Families Below Poverty Level, Female Heads	28.6%	73.9%

SOURCE: U.S. Bureau of the Census, Census of Population: 1970, Texas and Massachusetts.

an alternative to jobs with substandard wages while the less generous Houston system tends to sustain the availability of a cheap labor supply.

Summary

The most striking difference that emerges when one compares the Houston and Boston metropolitan areas is in terms of the relative proportions of their populations residing in the central city. Only 23 percent of the Boston SMSA's population is in the central city while for Houston the proportion is 62 percent. In addition, the legal and political fragmentation characteristic of Boston results in nearly two-thirds of its jobs being located outside the central city proper while for Houston it is less than 10 percent. Both cities have substantial black populations. However, Houston also has a large Hispanic population and Boston's white population is much more ethnically diverse than Houston's.

In terms of political culture, Boston is a more liberal
and progressive city than Houston and its racial attitudes are
relatively more accommodative. Employment growth in the Boston labor market was modest in recent years while employment
in Houston has grown at a phenomenal rate. Ethno-sex characteristics of the labor force and labor force participation
rates are basically comparable. However, there is an important difference between the cities relative to the role of
welfare as an alternative to the labor market as a source of
income. A more generous system in Boston in terms of payment
levels and acceptance rates permits workers to use welfare as
an alternative to jobs with substandard wages while the less
generous Houston system tends to sustain the availability of
a cheap labor supply. The boundaries of the cities are quite
different and as a result there are differential patterns of
access to employment by inner city minorities, especially in
Boston along the Route 128 complex of electronics firms.

NOTES

1. We operationally define a metropolitan labor market as
    coterminous with the Standard Metropolitan Statistical
    Area. This conforms to the traditional concept of labor
    markets as geographical areas surrounding a major central
    business or industrial district. In addition, data col-
    lection by the federal government is usually based on the
    SMSA, thus our collection of pertinent information is fa-
    cilitated by our use of the designation. Except in New
    England, an SMSA is defined as a county or group of con-
    tiguous counties containing at least one city of 50,000
    inhabitants or more or two cities with a combined popula-
    tion of at least 50,000. In New England, towns and cities
    rather than counties are used as geographic components of
    the SMSA. Since we prefer to use counties as the geo-
    graphic units, in this study we use for Boston the New
    England Metropolitan State Economic Area.   (This classi-
    fication is also used by the National Center for Health
    Statistics in its reports on hospitals and nursing homes
    and by the Commerce Department in County Business
    Patterns.) In this study the Houston SMSA includes the
    counties of Brazoria, Ford Bend, Harris, Liberty and
    Montgomery. Boston includes Essex, Middlesex, Norfolk
    and Suffolk counties.
2. Ronald Abler and John S. Adams, A Comparative Atlas of
    America's Great Cities: Twenty Metropolitan Regions
    (Minneapolis: University of Minnesota Press, 1976).
3. Arnold Fleischman, "The Politics of Postwar Growth and
    Annexation in San Antonio" in David C. Perry and Alfred
    J. Watkins eds., The Rise of Sunbelt Cities (Beverly
    Hills, Calif.: Sage, 1977), pp. 151-168.

4. Stanley Friedlander, Unemployment in the Urban Core: An
    Analysis of Thirty Cities with Policy Recommendations
    (New York: Praeger, 1972), p. 37.
5. Ibid., p. 36.
6. The Implementation of CETA in Eastern Massachusetts and
    Boston, R & D Monograph 57 (Washington: U.S. Department
    of Labor, 1978), p. 13.
7. Nathan Kantrowitz, "Racial and Ethnic Residential Segre-
    gation: Boston, 1830-1970," The Annals 441 (January
    1979), pp. 41-54.
8. James P. Sterba, "Houston Tangles with Problems of
    Success," New York Times, December 16, 1977, p. B1.
9. Scores are based on 1974 Americans for Democratic Action
    (ADA) ratings for members of Congress from districts
    wholly or in part within the Houston and Boston SMSAs.
    For Houston, the Congressional Districts include 2, 22,
    7, 8, 9 and 18 and for Boston 3, 4, 5, 6, 7, 8, 9, 10,
    11, and 12. The ADA scores, which range from 0-100, with
    100 equaling complete liberalism, were determined for
    each congressperson and a mean score was calculated. For
    Boston, districts 3 and 5 were excluded because the mem-
    bers were newly elected and hence no ratings were avail-
    able for them in 1974 (1974 was selected as the most re-
    cent year for which ADA rankings were available). Con-
    gressional district data were derived from the Congres-
    sional District Data Book, 93rd Congress and ADA ratings
    from M. Barone, G. Ujifusa and D. Matthews, The Almanac
    of American Politics (Boston: Gambit, 1976).
10. Percentages calculated for the counties in the SMSA. It
    is the average for the counties in the SMSA. Election
    data from America Votes, Vol. 9, 1972 (Washington:
    Congressional Quarterly, 1972).
11. Peter A. Lupsha and William Siembieda, "The Poverty of
    Public Services in the Land of Plenty: An Analysis and
    Interpretation" in Perry and Watkins eds., The Rise of
    Sunbelt Cities, p. 185.
12. Sterba, "Houston Tangles with the Problems of Success."
13. Margaret K. Latimer, "Black Political Representation in
    Southern Cities: Election System and Causal Variables,"
    Urban Affairs Quarterly 15 (September 1979), pp. 65-86.
14. Edward Banfield and J. Q. Wilson, City Politics (New York:
    Vintage Books, 1963), pp. 151-67.
15. New York Times, November 10, 1977.
16. See for example Dale Hiestand, Economic Growth and Employ-
    ment Opportunity for Minorities (New York: Columbia Uni-
    versity Press, 1964). See also Hiestand and Dean Morse,
    Comparative Metropolitan Employment Complexes: New York,
    Chicago, Los Angeles, Houston, Atlanta (New York: Allan-
    held Osmun and Co., 1979).
17. Ibid.
18. A. Sorenson, K. Taeuber and J. Holingsworth, "Indexes of

Racial Residential Segregation for 109 Cities in the United States, 1940-70," Sociological Focus (April 1975). See also K. and A. Taeuber, Negroes in Cities (Chicago: Aldine, 1965).

19.   Friedlander, Unemployment in the Urban Core, pp. 69-78.

20.   M. Cohen, T. Nagel and T. Scanlon, Equality and Preferential Treatment (Princeton: Princeton University Press, 1977).

21.   Gerald Pomper, Voter's Choice: Varieties of American Electoral Behavior (New York: Harper & Row, 1975).

22.   Percentages based on total employed persons sixteen and older in professional, technical and kindred occupations. Data from U.S. Census, Characteristics of the Population, Texas and Massachusetts for the Houston and Boston SMSAs.

23.   Implementation of CETA in Eastern Massachusetts and Boston, p. 123.

24.   Digest of Education Statistics, 1975 Edition (Washington: Department of Health, Education and Welfare), p. 191.

25.   Andrew Brimmer, The Economic Position of Black Americans: 1976 (Washington: National Commission for Manpower Policy, 1976), pp. 31-32.

26.   David C. Perry and Alfred J. Watkins, "People, Profit and the Rise of Sunbelt Cities" in Perry and Watkins, The Rise of Sunbelt Cities, pp. 297-87.

27.   Friedlander, Unemployment in the Urban Core, p. 81.

28.   Perry and Watkins, "People, Profit and the Rise of Sunbelt Cities," pp. 297-98.

CHAPTER 3
The Health and Electrical
Manufacturing Industries

In Chapter 2, we presented an analysis of the socio-economic, political, cultural and labor market characteristics of
the Houston and Boston metropolitan areas. In this chapter
the focus shifts to characteristics of the two industries.
The structures of the health and electrical manufacturing industries are examined in order to develop a descriptive and
contextual basis for consideration in the following chapter of
factors shaping black and female access to employment opportunities in the industries.

Employment Characteristics of the Houston and Boston Labor
Markets: 1975-79

As we noted in the previous chapter, employment has declined in Boston in recent years while Houston has experienced
phenomenal employment growth in the last 20 years. In Table
3.1 data on employment growth (excluding agriculture and self-
employment) are presented for Houston and Boston for the
period 1975-79. The table shows that employment by establishments in the Houston SMSA increased by 20.5 percent in the last
five years, up by 267,200 from 1,032,500 in 1975 to 1,299,700
in 1979. In Boston while the growth has not been as rapid as
in Houston, there has been a reversal of the pattern of decline
observed in recent years. Between 1975 and 1979, employment in
Boston grew by 7.9 percent, up by 109,300 from 1,259,800 to
1,369,100. Thus, in terms of the most basic difference between
the labor markets, rapid versus slow growth, the two economies
performed in the most recent period as they have throughout the
period of our study, 1965-75.

31

TABLE 3.1

MANUFACTURING EMPLOYMENT BY ESTABLISHMENTS,

HOUSTON AND BOSTON, 1975-79*

	1975	1979	% Change
Houston	1,032,500	1,299,700	20.5
Boston	1,259,800	1,369,100	7.9

*1975 figure is the annual average, 1979 figure is as of March 1979.

SOURCE: Bureau of Labor Statistics.

Average weekly earnings in the manufacturing sector and the cost of living in the two labor markets also varies. The Bureau of Labor Statistics (BLS) reports that the cost of an "Intermediate Level of Living" for a family of four in 1978 was $17,114 in Houston, up from $10,270 in 1972. In Boston a similar standard of living in 1978 required earning $22,117, up from $13,576 in 1972. Thus it costs considerably more to live in Boston than in Houston; however, average wages are lower in Boston than they are in Houston. According to BLS, in 1972 weekly earnings in manufacturing were $212.00 in Houston but only $195.00 in Boston, compared to $193.20 nationally. Thus in terms of wages and the cost of living, the Houston labor market is the more desirable one in which to live and work for the average employed blue collar worker.

The Health Industry

In a 1976 special report the National Commission for Man-power Policy reported that between 1960 and 1970 the number of employees in the health sector expanded from 2.6 million to 4.3 million, an increase of almost 65 percent. Nationally during this period, approximately 13 percent - one out of every eight - of all new jobs created were in this industry.[1] The Commission further reported that the health sector "provides a higher proportion of jobs than does the economy as a whole to black men and women, to Spanish heritage men, and most strikingly to women of all races, who account for almost three quarters of the employed health sector labor force at the same time that they represent less than 40 percent of the total labor force of the nation."[2]   Thus, the health sector is a growth industry and, in the past, receptive to historically disadvantaged workers.[3]

While there has been some slowdown in the rate of growth in the health sector in recent years, Table 3.2 shows that in Houston and Boston there has been continuing growth in the most recent period.

TABLE 3.2

EMPLOYMENT IN THE HEALTH INDUSTRY,

HOUSTON AND BOSTON, 1970-75*

	1970	1975	% Change
Houston	30,373	44,668	47.1
Boston	85,277	108,098	26.8

*Total employees is the count of employees during the pay period of mid-March as reported on Treasury Form 941, "Schedule A" or as corrected by estimates in those cases where it was improperly or incompletely reported.

SOURCE: U.S. Bureau of the Census, County Business Patterns, 1970, 1975.

In Houston between 1970 and 1975 total employment grew by 47.1 percent and in Boston by 26.8 percent.   Thus, in the health sector, as in industry generally, Houston has experienced more rapid growth than Boston.   However, we should note that measured by number of employees, Boston's health sector is considerably larger than Houston's, 108,098 in 1975 compared to Houston's 44,668.

Turning from the size and growth of the sector, institutions that employ allied health manpower can be divided into three basic categories: hospitals, ambulatory facilities and nursing homes and related facilities. Using data compiled by the National Center for Health Statistics, we discuss the structure of the industry in terms of type of institutions, number of employees and type of ownership.

Table 3.3 presents data on the number of hospitals, nursing homes and related facilities, percentage of employees in
nursing homes and related facilities, and beds per 1,000 population in hospitals and nursing homes for the Houston and Boston metropolitan areas. As a percentage of full-time employees, the table shows that nursing homes and related facilities
employ 13 percent of the health sector labor force in Boston
and 9 percent in Houston.[4] Nationally, 15 percent of health
workers are employed in nursing homes and related facilities;
thus both cities generally are lower than the national percent.
Boston's nursing home sector is significantly larger than
Houston's, in part because of the larger size of its elderly
population. In Boston there are 9.3 nursing home beds per
1,000, in Houston 4.1 and there are 78 nursing homes and related facilities in Houston, 543 in Boston. Nursing homes
employ 13,983 full-time persons in Boston, and 3,980 in
Houston.

Examining nursing homes and related facilities by type
of ownership, Table 3.4 shows that in both cities the bulk of
such institutions are operated on a proprietary basis; 84
percent (3.3 beds per 1,000) in Houston, 85 percent (7.5 beds
per 1,000) in Boston. Only a miniscule proportion are government operated, 1 percent of the units in Houston, .04 beds
per 1,000 and 3 percent of the units in Boston, .4 beds per
1,000. The percent of units and beds per 1,000 in the nonprofit sector, while larger, do not constitute a significant
part of the industry in either city.

Turning to hospitals, Boston's hospital industry is much
larger than Houston's. Returning to Table 3.3, there are 127
hospital units in Boston and 8.5 beds per 1,000 (compared to
7 beds per 1,000 nationally) while in Houston there are only
66 units and 5.8 beds per 1,000. The data reported in Table
3.5 show that in both cities the public sector is relatively
small; however, there is a major difference with respect to
the relative proportion of units and beds in the nonprofit
and proprietary sectors.

In Boston 70 percent of the units and 7.2 beds per 1,000
are in the nonprofit sector. In Houston 60 percent of the
units are in the proprietary sector; however, measured by
beds per 1,000 the nonprofit and proprietary sectors are
roughly comparable, 2.1 beds per 1,000 in the former and 2.2
per 1,000 in the latter.

According to the National Commission for Manpower Policy
"coverage under collective bargaining agreements is by no means
the rule for hospital workers but is becoming more and more
widespread, especially for registered nurses and for state and
local government."[5] The absence of strong trade union tradi-
tion in Texas and the South generally and the character of
Houston's civic culture leads us to expect a greater degree of

TABLE 3.3

SELECTED CHARACTERISTICS HEALTH CARE INDUSTRY,

HOUSTON AND BOSTON*

	Boston	Houston
Total Number of Hospitals	127	66
% Health Labor Force Employed in Hospitals	87	91
Beds Per Thousand Population	8.5	5.8
Total Number of Nursing Homes and Related Facilities	543	78
% Health Labor Force Employed in Nursing Homes	13	9
Beds Per Thousand Population	9.3	4.1

*Nursing home data are for 1973, and for hospitals, 1974.

SOURCES: Hospitals: A County and Metropolitan Area Data Book (Hyattsville, Md.; National Center for Health Statistics, 1977) and Nursing Homes: A County and Metropolitan Area Data Book (Hyattsville, Md.: National Center for Health Statistics, 1977).

TABLE 3.4

NURSING HOMES AND RELATED FACILITIES BY TYPE OF

OWNERSHIP, HOUSTON AND BOSTON, 1973

	Houston		Boston	
	% of Units	Bed per 1000	% of Units	Bed per 1000
Government	1	.04	3	.4
Proprietary	84	3.2	85	7.5
Nonprofit	15	.71	12	1.3

SOURCE: Nursing Homes: A County and Metropolitan Area Data Book, 1973 (Hyattsville, Md.: National Center for Health Statistics, 1977).

TABLE 3.5

HOSPITALS BY TYPE OF OWNERSHIP,

HOUSTON AND BOSTON, 1974

| | Houston | | Boston | |
	% of Units	Beds per 1000	% of Units	Beds per 1000
Government	12	1.0	22	1.0
Proprietary	60	2.2	8	.15
Nonprofit	16	2.1	70	7.2

SOURCE: Hospitals: A County and Metropolitan Area Data Book (Hyattsville, Md.: National Center for Health Statistics, 1977).

unionization in Boston than in Houston in both the public and private sectors.

The Bureau of Labor Statistics' survey of wages in the hospital industry does not report data on unionization in Houston or any other southern city except Memphis. However, the data on Boston show considerable collective bargaining coverage for workers in government and nongovernment hospitals. In Boston, among registered professional nurses, 20-23 percent are covered by collective bargaining agreements in nongovernment hospitals; 90-94 percent in state and local government hospitals; 10-14 percent of other professional and technical employees are covered in the private sector; 25-29 percent in the public sector; and among non-professional employees, 40-44 percent are covered in nongovernment hospitals and 85-89 percent in state and local government hospitals.[6]

The absence of data in the BLS survey from Houston and other southern cities is itself an indicator of the absence of unionization. The Service Employees International Union, a principal bargaining agent for hospital workers, has a thriving local in Boston but none in Houston. Thus the available data indicate that hospital employees are more unionized in Boston than they are in Houston.[7]

Workers in state and local government hospitals have enjoyed wide wage advantages over their counterparts in private hospitals but the gaps are narrowing. According to the BLS, between its first hospital wage survey in the mid-1960s and its most recent in 1972 "earning levels have usually risen at a faster pace for private than for government workers. The pay advantage for government workers has thus declined considerably in the last decade."[8] In its most recent survey, BLS reports that pay levels are usually highest in New York and San Francisco, lowest in Houston and other southern cities. In 1972, average weekly earnings for hospital workers in Boston were $177.71 compared to $151.94 in Houston. Workers in nongovernment hospitals in Boston were somewhat better paid than their counterparts in government hospitals - $180.72 in the former and $170.35 in the latter. In Houston the reverse is the case; nongovernment workers earn an average $142.63, government workers $155.74.[9] While hospital workers earn more in Boston, the differences are not so great when one recalls the cost of living in the two cities.

The Electrical Manufacturing Industry

The electrical and electronics manufacturing industry is a large and varied one.[10] Among its many products are transportation equipment (including parts for automobiles, trains, planes, boats and guided missiles), photographic equipment and supplies, household appliances, equipment and supplies for the development and utilization of electrical energy, surgical, medical and dental equipment and supplies and watches and clocks. The industry operates from huge factories with thousands of employees to small laboratory-like units that may employ less than a hundred persons. It includes some of the nation's largest corporations such as General Electric, RCA, Western Electric and Westinghouse but also relatively small firms that concentrate on the manufacture of small component parts.

It is a growth industry. Even with a relatively sharp increase in imports in recent years, domestic employment in the industry increased by more than a third between 1960-68, up by over a half million persons.[11] The proportion of white-collar or non-production workers is large and growing. In 1947 they constituted 22 percent of the industry work force, by 1976 this proportion was up to 32 percent.[12] Thus, we are dealing with a diversified and growing industry. Indeed, in the postwar period, 1947-60, employment in electrical equipment increased more than three times faster than in durable manufacturing, and made up 40 percent of the total net gain in jobs in the durable goods sector of the economy.[13]

In Table 3.6 data on employment and employment growth in the industry for Houston and Boston are presented. In terms of number of employees, the industry is much larger in Boston than in Houston. In 1975 there were 147,856 employees in the industry in Boston compared to 57,152 in Houston. But again, employment was up in Houston by 138.1 percent, 23.8 percent in

Boston. The rapid growth in Houston is no doubt in part a
function of the movement of some parts of the industry to the
South. Although recent employment data are not available, it
is estimated that the movement of jobs in the industry from
the Northeast to the South is considerable. For example, in
that part of the industry producing communications equipment
the Northeast lost 57,000 jobs between 1963-72 while the South
gained 38,000 (there was a net loss to the nation of 31,000
jobs). Thus by 1972 more than a quarter of the employees in
this part of the industry were located in the South; in 1963
only 15 percent of the employees were located there.[14]
However, we should note that in spite of the loss of manufacturing jobs in Boston and the northeast generally, in the most
recent period, 1970-75, the electrical manufacturing industry
in the city has grown at a respectable rate.

TABLE 3.6

EMPLOYMENT IN THE ELECTRICAL MANUFACTURING

INDUSTRY, 1970-1975*

	1970	1975	% Change
Houston	24,001	57,152	138.1
Boston	119,465	147,856	23.8

*Total employees is the count of employees during the pay
 period of mid-March as reported on Treasury Form 841
 "Schedule A" or as corrected by estimates in those cases
 where it was improperly or incompletely reported.

SOURCE: U.S. Bureau of the Census, County Business Patterns,
          1970, 1975.

The larger size of the industry in Boston is reflected in
other statistical data.   In Table 3.7 general statistics on
the industries of the two cities are presented. An inspection
of the table shows that measured by production workers, man-
hours, value added by manufacture, cost of materials, value of
shipments and capital expenditures the industry in Boston is
substantially larger than it is in Houston. For example, in
1972, 137.7 million man-hours were employed in Boston compared
to 55.9 in Houston. Materials in Boston cost more than one

and a half billion dollars, in Houston slightly more than a
half billion. Capital expenditures in 1972 were $110 million

TABLE 3.7

GENERAL STATISTICS, ELECTRICAL MANUFACTURING

INDUSTRY, 1972

	Boston	Houston
Production Workers (1000)	70.5	26.8
Man-Hours (millions)	137.7	55.9
Value Added by Manufacture (millions of dollars)	2458.7	798.2
Cost of Material (millions of dollars)	1552.0	542.2
Value of Shipments (millions of dollars)	3991.7	1297.2
Capital Expenditures (millions of dollars)	110.3	44.0

SOURCE: U.S. Bureau of the Census, Census of Manufactures,
          1972.

---

dollars in Boston, $44 million in Houston and the value added
in manufacture and the value of shipments were also two to
three times larger in Boston than Houston. In sum, a larger
more diversified industry in Boston and a faster growing one in
Houston.
     Reliable data on unionization are not available by city or
SMSA. The Bureau of Labor Statistics does not report extent
of coverage of collective bargaining agreements for the industry and the major unions are reluctant to divulge data on membership by city, state or region. The BLS reports that there
are 17 unions recognized as collective bargaining agents in
the industry. The largest are the International Union of
Electrical, Radio and Machine Workers (IUE) and the International Brotherhood of Electrical Workers (IBEW). Together
they enroll 60 percent of the workers in the industry.
     Previously, we suggested that Houston's conservative,
laissez-faire culture would depress unionization in the city.
Data on unionization in the health industry provide some support for this assumption. And the Directory of National and

International Unions reports the percentage of employees in
non-agricultural establishments with union membership for
Massachusetts at 25.6 percent and Texas at 14.4 percent.
Among the fifty states, Massachusetts ranks twenty-one, Texas,
forty-five. This suggests that the work force should be more
unionized in Boston than Houston.

In addition, unions in the industry have not been very
successful in organizing the growing work force. It is estimated that they have been able to add to their rolls only
about one production worker for every four net new jobs created in the electrical equipment sector of the industry.[15]
Union officials attribute this failure in part to the movement of workers to the South. As one official explained, "It
is difficult to organize these southern subsistence farms.
Their backgrounds help to explain it. The wages look good to
them and even better than good. They often travel long dis-
tances to get to work, still living on the farm. . . ."[16]
In addition, the more decentralized production characteristic
of the industry in the South is said to inhibit organizing.

Nevertheless, personal communications with the national
research departments of the major unions representing workers
in the industry indicate unionization is roughly the same in
the two cities. For example, IBEW reports that it has three
active locals in Houston, ten in Boston but that there is no
major difference between the two cities in terms of the extent of unionization. And the International Union of Electrical, Radio and Machine Workers reports it has little membership in the industry in Boston, and while there is some in
Houston this is more a function of the decline of the industry
in Boston than it is of differences in the degree of unionization.

Thus while we expected a more unionized work force in
Boston than Houston, the admittedly inadequate data available
indicate this is not the case in part perhaps because the
unions have concentrated their efforts on those large compa-
nies (General Electric, Westinghouse and Western Electric)
with whom they have national agreements.

Hourly earnings in the industry have lagged behind those
in durable manufacturing since 1960.[17] This is accounted
for in part by the relative share of women in the industry.
The share of women employed in the electrical equipment industry has for some time been about double the share in all
of the durable goods industries.[18] Since the earnings of
women almost always fall below those of men, the higher percentage of women in an industry, the lower the average earnings.
Within the electrical industry this pattern is quite pronounced. In 1975 those sectors with the most women had
average earnings 15 to 26 percent below the industry
average. The sectors with the lowest percent of women had
earnings at or above the industry wage (women predominate in
radio and television equipment, electronic components and

lighting wiring and equipment. The lowest proportion of women are in electrical test and distributing equipment, electrical industrial apparatus and household appliances).[19]

Looking at industry wages in Houston and Boston, in Table 3.8 average hourly earnings in manufacturing and electrical manufacturing are presented for Houston, Boston and the nation for 1975. In Boston the average earnings in the electrical manufacturing industry are $5.16 per hour, compared to $5.41 nationally in the industry, and $4.89 for manufacturing in the city and $4.83 for manufacturing nationally. Thus, a job in these industries in Boston pays less than the national average for the industries but more than the city average for manufacturing (27¢ per hour more) and more than the national average for manufacturing. In this context a job in Boston is a good job in terms of wages.

TABLE 3.8

AVERAGE HOURLY EARNINGS IN MANUFACTURING AND

ELECTRICAL MANUFACTURING, HOUSTON, BOSTON,

U.S.A., 1975

	Houston	Boston	U.S.A.
Manufacturing	$5.30	$4.89	$4.83
Electrical Manufacturing	-	$5.16	$5.41

*Average for electrical manufacturing includes SIC# 36, 37 and 38; data for SIC# 37 and 38 are not available for Houston.

SOURCE: Bureau of Labor Statistics.

In Houston, comparable data are not available. The BLS has average hourly earnings data for only one sector of the industry (SIC# 316), the electrical and electronic machinery equipment and supplies sector. While this sector is the lowest paid of the three, we can get some sense of the place of jobs in the industry in Houston by isolating this sector and comparing it with the same sector in Boston and in the nation as a whole. This is done in Table 3.9 below.

In Houston, workers in this sector average $4.00 per hour, compared to a national average of $4.64 in the sector and $4.83

TABLE 3.9

AVERAGE HOURLY EARNINGS MANUFACTURING AND ELECTRICAL -

ELECTRONIC EQUIPMENT MANUFACTURING, HOUSTON,

BOSTON, U.S.A., 1975

	Houston	Boston	U.S.A.
Manufacturing	$5.30	$4.89	$4.83
Electrical-Electronic Equipment Manufacturing	$4.00	$4.40	$4.64

SOURCE: Bureau of Labor Statistics

for all manufacturing nationally. Average hourly earnings in the manufacturing sector as a whole in Houston are $5.30 (compared to $4.89 in Boston). Thus jobs in this sector of the industry pay considerably less than the average manufacturing job in the city, $1.30 less. And the table shows that jobs in this sector pay more in Boston than in Houston, $4.40 compared to $4.00. It appears, then, that in spite of the higher average hourly earnings in manufacturing in Houston compared to Boston ($5.30 vs $4.89), workers in the electrical manufacturing sector do not do as well as their counterparts in Boston, at least this was the case in the lowest-paying sector. It appears that in the context of wages, jobs in the electrical manufacturing industry are not as good as the average manufacturing job in Houston and are less desirable than comparable jobs in Boston.

Summary

   Boston's labor market in terms of the number of jobs available is considerably larger than Houston's but jobs are increasing at a much faster rate in Houston. In the health and electrical manufacturing industries employment has increased in both cities but more rapidly in Houston than Boston. The health industry is larger in Boston and in both cities the public sector is relatively small; however, in Boston the nonprofit sector is dominant while in Houston, measured by beds per 1,000 population, the nonprofit and

proprietary sectors are roughly equivalent. Unionization is
prevalent in Boston's health sector and health workers earn
more in Boston than Houston; however, the differences are not
so great when considered in the context of the cost of living
in the two cities. The electrical manufacturing industry is
larger and more diversified in Boston. There appears to be no
difference in degree of unionization between the industries of
the cities; however, average earnings are higher in Boston
than they are in Houston relative to other manufacturing employment in the cities.

NOTES

1. Employment Impact of Health Policy Developments, Special
    Report No. 11 (Washington, D.C.: National Commission for
    Manpower Policy, 1976), p. 20.
2. Ibid., p. 21.
3. The Commission for Manpower Policy warns, "As health jobs
    become relatively more attractive and as jobs in the rest
    of the economy open up to more blacks and women, workers -
    particularly white men - who had, and even today continue
    to have, special advantages in the labor market may be
    expected to become increasingly interested in competing
    for health positions. . . . Thus it is possible that at
    the very time that wages and working conditions are im-
    proving, health care institutions may begin to favor
    those groups for whom other job opportunities in the
    economy have been most extensive and may begin to dis-
    criminate against their traditional employees (and indi-
    viduals with similar demographic characteristics)."
    Ibid., pp. 58-60.
4. These figures are approximate, based on 1973 data from
    Nursing Homes: A County and Metropolitan Area Data Book,
    1973 (Hyattsville, Md.: National Center for Health Sta-
    tistics, 1977) and 1975 data from County Business Pat-
    terns (Washington: U.S. Bureau of the Census, 1976).
5. Employment Impact of Health Policy Developments, p. 56.
6. Hospitals, Industry Wage Survey (Washington: Government
    Printing Office, 1975).
7. The American Federation of Teachers/AFL-CIO recently an-
    nounced a major organizing campaign aimed at nurses and
    health professionals throughout the country. The campaign
    will be directed by a new division within the union, the
    Federation of Nurses and Health Professionals (FNHP) AFT,
    AFL-CIO.
8. Hospitals, Industry Wage Survey, p. 4.
9. Ibid., p. 5.
10. The industry includes major group numbers 35, 36, 37 and
    38 in the Standard Industrial Classification Manual

(Washington: Executive Office of the President, 1972).
Much of the information in this chapter on the industry
is from James Kuhn's unpublished manuscript, "Collective
Bargaining in the Electrical Equipment Industry, 1970-77"
(Columbia University, Graduate School of Business Adminis-
tration, 1979).

11.   James Kuhn, "Collective Bargaining in the Electrical
      Equipment Industry, 1970-77," p. 12.
12.   Ibid., p. 5.
13.   Ibid.
14.   Ibid., p. 14.
15.   Ibid., p. 7.
16.   Ibid., p. 17.
17.   Ibid., p. 9.
18.   Ibid., p. 20.
19.   Ibid.

CHAPTER 4
Ethno-Sex Penetration of the Work Force

In the previous chapters, the structural characteristics of the cities and industries were described. In this chapter, the ethno-sex characteristics of the labor forces in the health and electrical manufacturing industries of Houston and Boston are examined. The participation of blacks and women in these industries in Houston and Boston is compared with their participation in "Other Industry" (all other industries excluding health and electrical manufacturing) and with their participation in the health, electrical manufacturing and other industries of the nation (excluding Houston and Boston). Throughout this chapter and the one that follows on mobility, the concept of "proportionate share" is used as a tool to analyze the participation of blacks and women in the labor force.

In the wake of the adoption of affirmative action as a principle of public policy in the United States by the federal executive, Congress, the courts and some state and local governments, there has emerged a small, largely polemical literature on the issue of the philosophy and efficacy of proportionality as a goal or means toward an eventual goal in the United States.[1] However, as an analytic tool, the concept predates the current controversy. In their classic, Black Metropolis, Drake and Cayton developed the term as a "device for comparing the occupational status of Negroes and whites by assuming: (1) that Negroes and whites have the same conception of what constitutes a 'good job'; (2) that Negroes, if permitted, would compete for these good jobs; (3) that there are no inherited mental differences between the races; (4) that if competition were absolutely unfettered by racial discrimination, Negroes, being approximately eight percent of the workers in 1930, would tend to approximate eight percent of each occupational group."[2]

 With the additional assumption that occupational differentials between black and white and male and female may, to
some extent, be related to educational attainments, we adopt
the Drake and Cayton method, while open to criticism, as the
theoretically most useful way to analyze the problem of employment discrimination and opportunity in the United States.
 In order to establish a base line for assessing group
shares and comparing the two cities, data on the labor force
participation rates of the ethno-sex groups are presented in
Table 4.1. The data are for 1970 because that year provides a
convenient midpoint between our three time periods, 1965, 1970
and 1975. Data for 1965 and 1975 are not available and while
1960 data are, it is preferable to use the 1970 figures because they are probably more reflective of the distribution in
1965 than are the 1960 data. The data show that blacks con-

TABLE 4.1

ETHNO-SEX GROUPS AS A PERCENT OF

THE LABOR FORCE, 1970[a]

	U.S.A.[b]	Boston	Houston
Whites	90%	96%	82%
Blacks	10%	4%	18%
Males	63%	59%	64%
Females	37%	41%	36%
Black Males	5.6%	2.1%	10%
Black Females	4.4%	1.9%	8%
White Males	57%	57%	54%
White Females	33%	39%	28%

(a) Data are for persons 16 years old and over.

(b) Data for blacks include other non-whites. Blacks constitute approximately 90% of the category.

SOURCES: U.S. Department of Labor, Bureau of Labor Statistics
 and U.S. Bureau of the Census, Census of the Population, 1970, Vol. 1, Characteristics of the Population, Part 23, Massachusetts, Part 45, Texas,
 Sections 1 and 2.

stitute about 10 percent of the labor force of the nation, women 37 percent, black males 5.6 percent, black females 4.4 percent and white females 33 percent.   In Boston, blacks constitute approximately 4 percent of the labor force, black males 2.1 percent, black females 1.9 percent and white females 38 percent.   And in Houston blacks are 18 percent, women 36 percent, black males 10 percent, black women 8 percent and white women 28 percent.   Given these approximate distributions, we turn first to consideration of ethno-sex penetration in the general industrial labor force, excluding health and electrical manufacturing.

Other Industry

U.S.A.

In Table 4.2, data on the penetration of the ethno-sex groups in the work force of the nation are presented for 1965, 1970 and 1975.   An inspection of the table reveals that in the

TABLE 4.2

ETHNO-SEX PENETRATION OF OTHER INDUSTRY, U.S.A.,

1965, 1970, 1975

	1965	1970	1975
Whites	88%	88.4%	89.1%
Blacks	12%	11.6%	10.9%
Males	62.9%	60.4%	66%
Females	37.1%	39.6%	34%
Black Males	6.7%	5.9%	6.1%
Black Females	5.3%	5.7%	4.8%
White Males	56.2%	54.5%	59.9%
White Females	31.8%	33.9%	29.2%

ten-year period, 1965-1975, the percentage of blacks and women employed in the nation's industries other than health and electrical manufacturing declined, from 12 percent to 10.9 percent and 37.1 percent to 34 percent respectively.   For blacks the decline was unaffected by time.   That is, the decline occurs in both time periods; however, for women there was an increase in the period 1965-70 from 37.1 percent to

39.6 percent and then, in the most recent period, a decline to 34 percent.   Thus, for women the period 1965-70 was one of growth while 1970-75 represents one of decline.   Overall, in the ten-year period, whites and males increased their share of available employment.

Examining the data in more detail, the decline among black males is observed only in the period 1965-70, with slight growth during 1970-75, although not enough to equal their share of 1965.   For black women, the period 1965-70 represents a period of modest growth, but during 1970-75 they fall below their share of 1965.   Thus, in the period of an expanding economy, 1965-70, women, black and white, made modest gains at the expense basically of white males; however, in the 1970-75 period of slow growth and recession white males recovered so that by the end of the period they had increased their share by more than 3 percent over 1965.

In relationship to distribution in the labor force, a somewhat different picture emerges.   Whites, approximately 90 percent of the labor force, held a 88 percent share of employment in 1965 and by 1975 this increased to 89.1 percent.   Conversely, blacks at 10 percent of the labor force held a 12 percent share in 1965, but by 1975 this declined to 10.9 percent.   This, to some extent, may reflect the decline in black participation in the labor force.   In 1963, 83 percent of blacks 16 and older were in the labor force, but by 1975 this had declined to 72 percent.   The white rate also declined but more modestly, from 83 percent to 79 percent.   Nevertheless, in 1975 blacks with 10 percent representation in the labor force held a rough proportionate share of employment.

Women constitute 37 percent of the labor force and their share of employment was 37.1 percent in 1965, 39.6 percent in 1970, but by 1975 their share fell to 34 percent, 3 percent below proportional representation.   Men, 63 percent of the labor force, held a 62.9 percent share in 1965, 60.4 percent in 1970, but 66 percent in 1975.   It is unclear whether these changes are a result of a decline in female labor force participation or of other factors.   But, whatever the reasons, it is clear that women lost shares of employment to men during the decade.

This is fundamentally a problem of white females because black women, 4 percent of the labor force, held a 5.3 percent share in 1965, 5.8 percent in 1970 and 4.8 percent in 1975, suggesting rough proportional representation.   Similarly, black males, 5.6 percent of the labor force, held a 6.7 percent share in 1965, 5.9 percent in 1970 and 6.1 percent in 1975. White males, 57 percent of the labor force, held a 56.1 percent share in 1965, 54.5 percent in 1970 and 59.9 percent in 1975. These data suggest two things.   First, white women during the ten-year period lost shares to white males, falling below proportional representation while the other groups were able to maintain proportional representation in spite of some losses. Second, 1965-70 was a period of increasing opportunities for women but 1970-75 saw most of these gains disappear while for blacks growth occurred in 1970-75 and declined in 1965-70.

Houston

In Table 4.3, participation data by ethno-sex group in the industry of Houston, excluding health and electrical manufacturing, are presented. The data show that, unlike in the nation where white women lost ground vis-à-vis white men in the decade, in Houston blacks lost ground to whites, male and female. In 1965, blacks, approximately 18 percent of the labor force, held exactly 18 percent of the jobs in Houston. But by 1970 their share declined to 15.6 percent and

TABLE 4.3

ETHNO-SEX PENETRATION OF OTHER INDUSTRY,

HOUSTON, 1965, 1970, 1975

	1965	1970	1975
Whites	82%	84.4%	85.9%
Blacks	18%	15.6%	14.1%
Males	69.4%	66.3%	69.3%
Females	30.6%	33.7%	30.7%
Black Males	10.3%	7.4%	7.5%
Black Females	7.7%	8.2%	6.6%
White Males	59.1%	58.9%	61.8%
White Females	22.9%	25.5%	24.4%

by 1975 to 14.1 percent. Conversely, whites increased their share from 82 percent to 85.9 percent. For black males the decline was most precipitate in the period 1965-70. With 10 percent of the labor force in 1965, they held a 10.3 percent share of employment but by 1970 this declined to 7.4 percent, increasing modestly to 7.5 percent by 1975. Black women, on the other hand, 8 percent of the labor force, in 1965 held a 7.7 percent share and this increased to 8.2 percent by 1970. However, by 1975 this share decreased to 6.6 percent. Thus while both groups lost shares during the ten year period, there is a major difference with respect to time. For black men, the losses occur during the 1965-70 period of economic growth and

heightened civil rights activity. While for black women this
is a period of growth with the decline occurring during the
1970-75 period of declining civil rights activity and recession and slow growth.

White women, 36 percent of the labor force, made modest
gains in the 1965-70 period. Their share of employment increased from 22.9 percent to 25.5 percent, and declined
slightly during 1970-75 to 24.4 percent. Overall, then, unlike their black counterparts, white women registered some
gains in the ten-year period. The share of employment held by
white males, 54 percent of the labor force, in 1965 was 59.1
percent, down to 58.9 percent in 1970 but up to 61.8 percent
in 1975. Thus, in Houston, unlike the nation, white males
held a somewhat larger share of employment than their proportion in the labor force and during the ten-year period, after
some decline, this share increased slightly. The gains made by
whites, male and female, were made at the expense of blacks,
especially men. This differs from the national pattern, where
gains were made by white males at the expense of all other
groups.

Boston

In Boston we observe a pattern more akin to that in the
nation than Houston. The data reported in Table 4.4 show that
white women lost shares to white men during the decade. Approximately 39 percent of the labor force, white women constituted 36 percent of the industrial work force in 1965, up to
38 percent in 1970 but down sharply by 1975 to 30 percent, 6
percent below the 1965 level. The bulk of the losses by white

TABLE 4.4

ETHNO-SEX PENETRATION OF OTHER INDUSTRY

BOSTON, 1965, 1970, 1975

	1965	1970	1975
Whites	96%	95%	95%
Blacks	4%	5%	5%
Males	62%	60%	67%
Females	38%	40%	33%
Black Males	2%	2%	2%
Black Females	2%	3%	3%
White Males	60%	57%	65%
White Females	36%	38%	30%

women were the result of gains by white men. Approximately 57 percent of the labor force, in 1965 their share was 60 percent, down to 57 percent in 1970 but up to 65 percent by 1975. Thus the period 1965-70 was one of growth for white men but, in the 1970-75 period, the process is reversed with males making substantial gains at the expense of women.

Regarding blacks, approximately 4 percent of the labor force, and with 4 percent of the employment in 1965 they have exact parity and a 1 percent increase is observed between 1965-70. All of this increase is accounted for by females, approximately 2 percent of the labor force, their share of employment increases from 2 percent in 1965 to 3 percent in 1970. The male share remains unchanged at 2 percent, compared to their approximate 2.1 percent of the labor force. Thus the period 1965-70 is the significant time for black women (no change is observed for blacks, male or female, during 1970-75) with regard to penetration in Boston.

In summary, the Boston labor market provides blacks with a proportionate share of employment and more, while in the Houston labor market blacks begin in 1965 with a proportionate share but during the ten-year period lose ground to whites, such that by 1975 they are several points below parity. In the nation, blacks lost ground but nevertheless retain a proportionate share. In both Houston and Boston white women are below parity although some progress is observed in Houston while shares are lost in Boston and the nation. The affect of time varies by place and group. For blacks in Boston, 1965-70 is the critical period of growth but in Houston and the nation, this is a period of growth in all places while 1970-75 generally represents a period of decline.

Health

U.S.A.

As we indicated in Chapter 3, the health industry has historically been more open to blacks and women than other industries. The data reported in Table 4.5 below are consistent with this history. Given their percentages in the national labor force, blacks and women at all three measuring periods are well represented in the nation's health industry. This of course is especially the case for women, black and white, whose share of jobs in the industry is more than twice their percentage of the labor force.

There is evidence, however, that tends to provide support for the National Commission for Manpower Policy's 1976 warning that as wages and working conditions tend to improve in the industry blacks and women may lose their traditionally favored

position. While women did not lose shares in the ten years, blacks,
especially males, did lose shares. Blacks, approximately 10
percent of the labor force, in 1965 held a 15.7 percent share
of employment in the industry, in 1970 14.8 percent and 1975
13.6 percent. Most of these changes are a result of a decline
in shares held by black men, down from 3.9 percent in 1965 to
2.6 percent in 1975, with most of the loss occurring during
the period 1970-75 (black women declined between 1970-75 from
11.8 percent to 11 percent). White men and women gained about
equally as a result of the black loss, white males up from
15.8 percent to 16.8 percent, white women from 68.5 percent to
69.6 percent. Thus while blacks and women throughout held
more than a proportionate share of the industry's employment,
blacks, especially black men, lost some ground during the
decade, generally between 1970-75.

TABLE 4.5

ETHNO-SEX PENETRATION OF THE HEALTH INDUSTRY,

U.S.A., 1965, 1970, 1975

	1965	1970	1975
Whites	84.3%	85.2%	86.4%
Blacks	15.7%	14.8%	13.6%
Males	19.7%	17.3%	19.4%
Females	80.3%	82.7%	80.6%
Black Males	3.9%	3%	2.6%
Black Females	11.8%	11.8%	11%
White Males	15.8%	14.3%	16.8%
White Females	68.5%	70.9%	69.6%

Houston

In Table 4.6, the data on the ethno-sex distribution of
the work force in Houston are presented for the years 1965,
1970, and 1975. The table shows that women, already well represented in the industry, increased their share of employment,
while men, black and white, lost shares. For blacks, the decade 1965-75 shows steady growth, from 22.9 percent in 1965 to
28.1 percent in 1975. Women increased their share from 80.2
percent in 1965 to 84.8 percent in 1975. Thus, given their
proportion of the city's labor force (18 percent and 28 percent respectively) blacks and women have done quite well in
the Houston health labor market.

TABLE 4.6

ETHNO-SEX PENETRATION OF THE HEALTH INDUSTRY,

HOUSTON, 1965, 1970, 1975

	1965	1970	1975
Whites	77.1%	72.6%	71.9%
Blacks	22.9%	26.6%	28.1%
Males	19.8%	15.3%	15.2%
Females	80.2%	84.7%	84.8%
Black Males	5.8%	2.6%	3.2%
Black Females	17.1%	24%	24.9%
White Males	14%	12.7%	12%
White Females	63.1%	59.9%	59.9%

A closer study of Table 4.6 reveals that it is black women who have experienced the real increase in shares, from 17.1 percent in 1965 to 24.9 percent in 1975. All other ethno-sex groups show a loss in shares, white women down from 63.1 percent in 1965 to 59.9 percent in 1975, white men from 14 percent to 12 percent and black men from 5.8 percent to 3.2 percent. Thus, black women in the period 1965-75, were very successful in seeking employment in Houston's health industry.

Boston

If black women made gains in Houston such is not the case in Boston where the gains are made by men, black and white, at the expense of black and white women. The data are reported in Table 4.7. It shows that while blacks have a larger share of jobs in the industry than their proportion of the city's labor force (6 percent vs 4 percent), they lost ground in the course of the decade. In 1965, the black share was 6.6 percent; it increased to 7.4 percent by 1970, but declined by 1975 to 6.2 percent. The share held by black men increased modestly in the ten-year period, from 1.5 percent to 1.8 percent but the share by black women declined overall, moving up slightly in the period to 4.4 percent (although this share is well above their 1.9 percent share in this city's labor force). Thus, the Boston health labor market operated in a manner exactly opposite to Houston's, black women lost shares in the former during 1970-75 while they made considerable gains during this period in the former.

TABLE 4.7

ETHNO-SEX PENETRATION OF THE HEALTH INDUSTRY,

BOSTON, 1965, 1970, 1975

	1965	1970	1975
Whites	93.4%	92.6%	93.8%
Blacks	5.5%	7.4%	6.2%
Males	20.5%	21.1%	23.7%
Females	79.5%	78.9%	76.3%
Black Males	1.5%	1.7%	1.8%
Black Females	5.1%	5.7%	4.4%
White Males	19%	19.4%	21.9%
White Females	74.4%	73.2%	71.9%

The share of jobs held by white women also declined, from 74.4 percent in 1965 to 71.9 percent in 1975. Therefore, the group that gained was males, blacks up marginally but white males up from 19.1 percent to 21.9 percent. Thus the Boston labor market operated to increase shares for males, black and white, at the expense of women.

In summary, while blacks and women in Houston, Boston and the nation hold more than their share of health employment, we observe different patterns of change for the groups depending on time and place. In the nation, blacks, especially males, lost shares during 1970-75 to whites; in Houston black women gained shares in 1965-70 at the expense of males, black and white, and in Boston women, black and white, lost shares to males, especially white, during the period 1970-75.

Electronics

U.S.A.

Unlike the health industry, white males dominate the electronics and electrical manufacturing industry. In Table 4.8 data on the ethno-sex distribution of the work force in the industry are presented. In 1965, blacks held a 5.4 percent share of industry employment and by 1975 this share had increased to 8.4 percent. A respectable increase but not enough to achieve proportional representation. Women increased their share from 21.3 percent in 1965 to 24.5 percent in 1970 and then dropped slightly to 24.4 percent by 1975 (the share held

TABLE 4.8

ETHNO-SEX PENETRATION OF THE ELECTRICAL

MANUFACTURING INDUSTRY, U.S.A.

1965, 1970, 1975

	1965	1970	1975
Whites	94.6%	92.3%	91.6%
Blacks	5.4%	7.7%	8.4%
Males	78.7%	75.3%	75.6%
Females	21.3%	24.5%	24.4%
Black Males	4.3%	5.6%	5.9%
Black Females	1.1%	2.1%	2.5%
White Males	74.4%	69.9%	69.7%
White Females	20.2%	22.4%	21.9%

by black women increases steadily from 1.1 percent in 1965 to
2.5 percent in 1975). Again, this represents some modest im-
provement but women remain more than 10 percent below their
proportional share. For women, the period 1965-70 was the
time of growth while for blacks growth was steady in both periods. In general, then, white males lost shares of employment
in the industry during the decade (down from 74.4 percent in
1965 to 69.7 percent in 1975) to blacks and women but nevertheless continue to dominate the industry, 69.7 percent of industry employment compared to 57 percent of the labor force.

Houston

In Table 4.9 ethno-sex data on employment in electrical
manufacturing in Houston are presented. As in the nation, the
industry in Houston is dominated by white males, but women and
blacks have increased their shares in the industry with blacks
achieving proportional representation by 1975. In 1965, white
males held 82.2 percent of employment but by 1975 this share
declines to 71.4 percent. During this period black males increased their share of employment from 7.1 percent to 11.2
percent, white females from 10.7 percent to 15.8 percent and
black females from no representation in 1965 to a modest 1.6
percent by 1975. Thus, by the end of our study period, black
males achieve and exceed their proportional share in the industry, white females made progress but were more than 10 per-

TABLE 4.9

ETHNO-SEX PENETRATION OF THE ELECTRICAL

MANUFACTURING INDUSTRY, HOUSTON,

1965, 1970, 1975

	1965	1970	1975
Whites	92.9%	87.6%	87.2%
Blacks	7.1%	12.4%	12.8%
Males	89.3%	85.9%	82.6%
Females	10.7%	14.1%	17.4%
Black Males	7.1%	10.7%	11.2%
Black Females	0	1.7%	1.6%
White Males	82.2%	75.2%	71.4%
White Females	10.7%	12.4%	15.8%

cent below parity in 1975 and black women barely achieve entry
by 1975. Progress for blacks and women was steady throughout
although blacks made their major gains in the period 1965-70
while women (largely white) made more progress in the period
1970-75.

Boston

The Boston pattern differs somewhat from that of Houston
although there are similarities. The data reported in Table
4.10 show that in the decade 1965-75 blacks and women gained
shares of employment and white males lost shares. In 1965,
blacks held a 2.5 percent share, by 1975 they achieve proportional representation, 4.1 percent of the industry compared to
4 percent of the labor force. Women increased their share from
30.1 percent in 1965 to 31.6 percent in 1975. In sum, white wom-
en really stood still in the ten-year period while blacks,
males and female, made substantial gains, with black males exceeding parity and black women achieving near parity. White
women still lag behind their proportion in the labor force
(31.6 percent vs 39 percent) thus white males have a larger
share of employment than their proportions in the labor force
as a result of the underrepresentation of women.

TABLE 4.10

ETHNO-SEX PENETRATION OF THE ELECTRICAL

MANUFACTURING INDUSTRY, BOSTON,

1965, 1970, 1975

	1965	1970	1975
Whites	97.5%	96.9%	94.9%
Blacks	2.5%	3.1%	4.1%
Males	68.5%	70.2%	66.8%
Females	31.5%	29.7%	33.2%
Black Males	1.1%	1.7%	2.5%
Black Females	1.4%	1.4%	1.6%
White Males	67.4%	68.5%	64.3%
White Females	30.1%	28.3%	31.6%

Summary

Blacks and women find more employment opportunities in the health industry than in other industries generally or in the electrical manufacturing industry specifically. However, compared to other industries, blacks and women are underrepresented in the electrical manufacturing industry. Generally, the Boston labor market provides more employment opportunities for blacks and women than does Houston's or the nation's and, while there are variations by place, industry, and group, generally the period 1965-70 is the most productive in terms of expanding employment opportunities.
The data on the penetration of blacks and women in the category of other industry in the United States, Houston and Boston in the decade 1965-1975 show that for blacks the Boston labor market that provides increased shares of employment while their share of employment declines in the nation and in Houston. The percentage of blacks in 1975 employed in the other industry category of Boston exceeds their proportion of the labor force, while in the nation it is roughly equivalent, and in Houston the black share is down from a proportional 18 percent in 1965 to 14 percent in 1975. Yet during this ten-year period, employment growth in Houston is estimated at 106 percent, while in Boston it is a modest 19 percent, suggesting that growth in employment is not the central factor

in enhanced black access to employment opportunities. The
case of women is somewhat different; in both the nation and
Boston, their share of employment declines, while in Houston it
is unchanged, indicating again the marginal impact of rapid
employment growth on the employment opportunities of the disadvantaged.

The penetration data on blacks and women in the health
and electrical manufacturing industries reveal a somewhat similar pattern. First, in both industries the growth in employment is substantially greater in Houston than in Boston.   In
the Houston health industry both blacks and women increased
their share of employment, while in Boston their shares decline
during the decade. In the electrical manufacturing industry
increasing shares for blacks and women are observed in both
cities; however, it is in Boston rather than Houston where the
greater degree of penetration is observed. In Boston blacks
are proportionally represented in the industry, women are near
proportional representation but in Houston both groups are
substantially below proportional representation.

In general, then, the cautious conclusion is that employment growth per se is not the decisive factor in black and female access to employment opportunities. Given Houston's
phenomenal growth rate compared to Boston's, one would have
anticipated more access by blacks and women to employment in
Houston than in Boston but this is not the case, suggesting
that other factors in addition to growth are important determinants of employment opportunities for women and blacks.
Among these other factors, women and blacks in Boston were ap-
parently aided by relatively more favorable attitudes and administrative procedures and processes and were not as much
aided by growth as their counterparts were in Houston.   But
the net result was not far different in the two quite different cities and labor markets.

NOTES

1.   Nathan Glazer, Affirmative Discriminiation: Ethnic In-
     equality and Public Policy (New York: Basic Books, 1975);
     Stanley Masters, Black-White Income Differentials: Empir-
     ical Studies and Policy Implications (New York: Academic
     Press, 1975); Alan Sindler, Bakke, DeFunis and Minority
     Admissions Inequality and Affirmative Action (San Fran-
     cisco: W.H. Freeman, 1979); Joel Dreyfuss and Charles
     Lawrence, The Politics of Inequality (New York: Harcourt
     Brace, 1979); Richard Lester, Reasoning About Discrimina-
     tion: The Analysis of Professional and Executive Work in
     Federal Antibias Programs (Princeton, N.J.: Princeton

University Press, 1980) and Edwin Dorn, Rules and Racial
Inequality (New Haven: Yale University Press, 1979).
2. St. Clair Drake and Horace Cayton, Black Metropolis (New
York: Harcourt Brace, 1945), p. 218.

CHAPTER 5
Ethno-Sex Mobility in the Work Force

In this chapter we trace the mobility of the ethno-sex groups in the health and electrical manufacturing industries of Houston and Boston compared to "Other Industry" in these cities and the health, electrical manufacturing and "Other Industry" of the nation. By mobility we mean progress through income categories in the periods 1965-1970 and 1970-75. The income categories, adjusted for inflation, are low (up to $5,999), middle ($6.000-$14,999) and high ($15,000 and over). As in Chapter 4, the concept of proportionate share is employed as the basic tool of analysis.

Other Industry

U.S.A.

The data on mobility of ethno-sex groups in other industries of the United States are presented in Table 5.1. The data show that in 1965 blacks and women were concentrated in the low income categories while white males predominated in the middle and high income categories. For example, white men, approximately 56 percent of the industry work force, held 91 percent of the middle income employment, 99.3 percent of the high but only 47.2 percent of the low. Blacks, on the other hand, about 12 percent of the work force, held 14.2 percent of low income employment, 3.7 percent of middle and only .2 percent of the high. And women, 37 percent of the industry, held 45.2 percent of low income employment but only 5.3 percent and .5 percent of middle and high income employment.

During the ten years, blacks and women made some progress through income categories, especially at the middle level, but not enough to achieve anything near their proportionate shares

TABLE 5.1

ETHNO-SEX MOBILITY, OTHER INDUSTRY, U.S.A.,

1965, 1970, 1975

	1965			1970			1975		
	Low	Mid	High	Low	Mid	High	Low	Mid	High
Blacks	14.2%	3.7%	.2%	15.2%	7.4%	1.1%	15.1%	11.1%	3.7%
Males	7.6%	3.5%	.2%	6.4%	5.8%	1.0%	6.5%	6.9%	3.2%
Females	6.6%	.2%	0	8.8%	1.6%	.1%	8.6%	4.2%	.5%
Whites	85.8%	96.3%	99.8%	84.8%	92.5%	98.9%	84.9%	88.9%	96.3%
Males	47.2%	91%	99.3%	36.7%	77.8%	97%	35.3%	62.4%	92.2%
Females	38.6%	5.3%	.5%	48.1%	14.8%	1.9%	49.6%	26.5%	4.1%

in the upper-income categories. In 1975 whites still held
96.3 percent of upper income jobs and white males held a 92.2
percent share. Thus blacks, approximately 10 percent of the
industry, were able to command only a 3.7 percent share of upper income employment, all save .5 percent held by men. Similarly, women with about a third of the industry work force
held but 4.1 percent of the best paying jobs, compared to 58
percent of the low paying ones. Thus after a decade of much
agitation concerning equal employment opportunity, United
States industry at its apex remains dominated by white males.

Blacks did make some progress at the middle level of employment, increasing from 3.7 percent in 1965 to 11.1 percent
in 1975. Given their participation in the industry, this figure represents a proportionate share. Unlike the growth in
high income employment where black males were the principal
beneficiary, in the middle income category black males and females share about equally in the growth.

With respect to white women, a similar pattern is observed. From a 5.3 percent share in 1965 to a 26.5 percent
share in 1975. This represents considerable progress although,
unlike blacks, it does not represent a proportionate share.

In sum, nationally white males continue to dominate upper
income employment but in both time periods steady progress is
observed for blacks and women at the middle level such that
the white male share declines from 91 percent in 1965 to 62.4
percent in 1975.

Houston

In Table 5.2, data on mobility in other industries of
Houston are presented. The Table shows with respect to high
income employment a pattern similar to that observed for the
nation, dominance by white males. However, in Houston this
dominance, given the black proportion of the industry, is even
more pronounced. In 1965 and again in 1970 white males held
100 percent of measured employment. In the period 1970-75,
some progress is observed, the share held by males declines to
91.4 percent.

The black share in 1975 was 2.4 percent and unlike in the
nation in Houston black women share equally in this growth (the
share held by white women is 6.2 percent in 1975). Thus, with
respect to high income employment the Houston labor force is
even more the preserve of white males. We should also note
that no progress is observed in the fast growth 1965-70 period
but rather the latter period, 1970-75.

Looking at the middle income category, black mobility is
observed, from 4.6 percent to 15.2 percent between 1965 and
1975 which exceeds by a point their proportionate share. The
progress is most striking for black women; in 1965 no women are

TABLE 5.2

ETHNO-SEX MOBILITY, OTHER INDUSTRY, HOUSTON,

1965, 1970, 1975

	1965			1970			1975		
	Low	Mid	High	Low	Mid	High	Low	Mid	High
Blacks	23%	4.6%	0	23.9%	6.3%	0	24.3%	15.2%	2.4%
Males	12.5%	4.6%	0	9.7%	5.4%	0	13.5%	7.9%	1.2%
Females	10.5%	0	0	14.2%	.9%	0	10.8%	7.3%	1.2%
Whites	77%	95.4%	100%	76.1%	93.7%	100%	75.7%	84.8%	97.6%
Males	47%	92.3%	100%	37.4%	82.9%	100%	36.5%	58.5%	58.5%
Females	30%	3.1%	0	38.7%	10.8%	0	39.2%	26.3%	6.2%

represented in the middle income category, in 1970 .9 percent, but between 1970-75 remarkable progress is observed as they achieve a 7.3 percent share which exceeds their proportionate share. Black men in 1965 held a 4.6 percent share and this increases steadily in both time periods to 7.9 percent, slightly better than proportionality. Thus, while blacks are overrepresented in low income category and underrepresented in the high, by 1975 they are proportionally represented in the middle sector. Again, it is interesting to observe that middle sector mobility in Houston is more pronounced in the 1970-75 period rather than the rapid growth 1965-70 period, especially insofar as black women are concerned.

     For women steady movement is observed in the middle sector during both periods, 3.1 percent in 1965, 10.8 percent in 1970 and 26.3 percent in 1975 (2 percent above their proportionate share). As a result, the share of middle sector employment held by white males declines from 92.3 percent in 1965 to 58.5 percent in 1975. Nevertheless, in sum, the data reveal a continued disparate affect, white males represented disproportionately in high income employment, blacks and women in the low income. Only in the middle income sector is significant progress toward equal employment opportunity observed.

     Boston

     In Boston, we observe somewhat different patterns than those observed in Houston and the nation, although there are similarities in terms of middle sector mobility. The data are presented in Table 5.3 and it reveals that like Houston and the nation, white males predominate in the upper income category, blacks and women in the low income category. In 1965 and 1970 whites held 100 percent of measured high income employment. Some mobility is observed in the 1970-75 period such that by 1975 blacks hold a 2 percent share (1.5 percent male, .5 percent female) of high income employment. In 1975, blacks constituted approximately 5 percent of other industry workers in Boston (2 percent male, 3 percent female); thus the 1.5 black male share is approaching proportionality while black women lag considerably behind.

     With respect to white women in the high income category, we observe no representation in 1965, 3 percent in 1970 and 4 percent in 1975. Women constitute 30 percent of the industry, thus they are severely underrepresented in this category.

     In the middle income category, blacks, male and female, achieve proportional representation by 1970 and exceed it by two points in 1975, 5 percent of industry work force but 7 percent of middle income employment. And by 1975, black males are no longer overrepresented in the low-income segment

TABLE 5.3

ETHNO-SEX MOBILITY, OTHER INDUSTRY, BOSTON,

1965, 1970, 1975

	1965			1970			1975		
	Low	Mid	High	Low	Mid	High	Low	Mid	High
Blacks	5%	2%	0	7%	4%	0	5%	7%	2%
Males	3%	2%	0	2%	3%	0	1%	4%	1.5%
Females	2%	0	0	5%	1%	0	4%	3%	.5%
Whites	95%	98%	100%	93%	96%	100%	95%	93%	98%
Males	50%	95%	100%	36%	80%	97%	39%	62%	94%
Females	45%	3%	0	57%	16%	3%	56%	31%	4%

and black women only marginally.

White women move from a 3 percent middle sector share in 1965, 16 percent in 1970 and 31 percent in 1975, representing a proportionate share. However, unlike blacks, women remain disproportionately represented in the low-income segment.

In sum, then, the pattern in Boston resembles that in Houston and the nation insofar as middle sector employment is concerned, however, blacks, male and female, experience greater mobility in all income segments in Boston than they do in Houston or the nation, although black women experience substantially more mobility in Houston than they do in the nation. In Boston (except for black high income mobility) and the nation, mobility is observed in both the 1965-70 and the 1970-75 periods while in Houston more progress, especially for black women, is observed in the 1970-75 period.

Health

U.S.A.

As in industry generally in the nation and in Houston and Boston, Table 5.4 reveals that white men dominate the upper income category of health industry employment. But given the share of employment held by blacks and women in the health industry, the disparate affect is particularly striking. In 1965, the white share of upper income employment was 99.5 percent, 1970 96.4 percent and 1975 95 percent. Of this share, white males in 1965 held 92.5 percent, in 1970 84.8 percent and in 1975 72.3 percent. This suggests some mobility, largely for white females, during the ten years but given their 69.6 percent share of jobs in the industry, their 22.7 percent of high income jobs is far less than parity (females tend to be nurses in this category rather than physicians). And blacks have fared no better, with a 13.6 percent share of jobs in the industry they hold but a 5 percent share of the best paying jobs.

The movement of women and blacks into the high income category was observed in both time periods. Black women were slightly more mobile than black men, moving from zero in 1965 to 2.9 percent in 1975, however, the 2.1 percent share held by black men is almost equal to their 2.6 percent share of the industry while the 2.9 percent share held by black women is far below their 11 percent share of the industry. In sum, with respect to high income employment, while some mobility for blacks and women is observed, white male dominance is still evident, constituting 16.8 percent of the industry work force but 72.3 percent of the best paying jobs.

Looking at the middle income sector, women, black and white, approach near parity during the decade with a consequent

TABLE 5.4

ETHNO-SEX MOBILITY, HEALTH, U.S.A.,

1965, 1970, 1975

	1965			1970			1975		
	Low	Mid	High	Low	Mid	High	Low	Mid	High
Blacks	16.7%	6.2%	.5%	16.7%	9.3%	3.6%	14.4%	13.9%	5%
Males	3.9%	3.7%	.5%	3%	3%	2.2%	2.4%	3%	2.1%
Females	12.8%	2.5%	0	13.7%	6.3%	1.4%	12.0%	10.9%	2.9%
Whites	84.3%	93.8%	99.5%	83.3%	90.7%	96.4%	85.6%	86.1%	95%
Males	11.2%	57.6%	92%	9.5%	24.3%	84.8%	10.3%	16.1%	72.3%
Females	72.1%	36.2%	7.5%	73.8%	66.4%	11.6%	75.3%	70%	22.7%

loss of shares by white males.   In 1965 blacks held a 6.2 percent share, in 1970 9.3 percent and in 1975 13.9 percent;
the share held by women, approximately two-thirds of the industry, increases from 36.2 percent in 1965 to 70 percent by
1975.   Thus progress is observed in both periods with blacks
and women achieving parity by 1975.   Most of the black mobility here is experienced by women since black men, ranging from
2.6 percent to 3.9 percent of the industry, held an approximate proportionate share of middle sector employment in all
periods.

Thus, nationally we observe three patterns in the health
industry.   In the high paying sector, white male dominance
despite some progress by blacks and women in the ten year period and considerable mobility into the middle sector with
blacks and women achieving parity by 1975.   White males are
underrepresented in the low income sector, blacks, male and
female, are at rough parity and white women remain somewhat
overrepresented.   Finally, mobility does not loom larger in
any particular time period, 1965-70 or 1970-75.

Houston

In Table 5.5 data on the income distribution of the ethno-
sex groups are presented.   Looking first at the blacks, in 1965
the entire black labor force in Houston's health industry was
employed in the low income segment.   During the decade blacks
made significant progress in penetrating the middle income
category but only modest progress in the high income sector.

In the middle sector, the black share increased from zero
in 1965 to 8.8 percent in 1970 and then increased dramatically
to 23.2 percent in 1975, compared to their 28.1 percent of the
industry.   Black women increased their share from zero to 20.3
percent and black men increased their share from zero to 2.9
percent.   This represents near parity for both groups although
black men, approximately three percent of the industry, are
nearer parity than black women, who constitute approximately
twenty-five percent of the industry.   The group in 1975 is
also disproportionately represented in the low income category,
increasing from 24.4 percent in 1965 to 35.3 percent in 1975.

In the high income sector, little mobility is observed
for blacks.   Black men began and ended the decade with no
representation in this category, while black women made modest
progress, from zero in 1970 to 3.4 percent in 1975.

White women begin in 1965 with good though not proportional representation in the middle income sector, 41.7 percent compared to 63.1 percent of industry employment.   In the ten year
period, this share increases to 67.1 percent, nearly five
points above parity.   In the high income sector, in 1965 no
white females were represented and no change is observed be-

TABLE 5.5

ETHNO-SEX MOBILITY, HEALTH, HOUSTON,

1965, 1970, 1975

	1965			1970			1975		
	Low	Mid	High	Low	Mid	High	Low	Mid	High
Blacks	24.4%	0	0	34.8%	8.8%	0	35.3%	23.2%	3.4%
Males	6.1%	0	0	3.3%	1%	0	3.8%	2.9%	0
Females	18.3%	0	0	31.5%	7.8%	0	31.5%	20.3%	3.4%
Whites	75.6%	100%	100%	65.2%	91.2%	100%	64.2%	76.8%	96.6%
Males	10.3%	58.3%	100%	6.2%	26.5%	100%	7.1%	9.1%	69%
Females	65.3%	41.7%	0	59.0%	64.7%	0	57.6%	67.1%	27.6%

tween 1965 and 1970, however, in the period 1970-75 considerable progress is observed so that by 1975 they constitute 27.6
percent of the segment, still considerably below parity but
nevertheless evidence of some mobility.

In Houston, then, the data reveal the following patterns.
First, white male dominance of the high and middle income jobs
at the beginning of the study period with a resulting disproportionate representation of blacks and women in the low income sector. Second, considerable mobility, approaching parity
and better, for blacks and women in the middle income sector.
Middle sector mobility for blacks was most pronounced in the
period 1970-75 and for women in the period 1965-70. Most of
the black mobility in this sector is accounted for by women who
constitute 20.3 percent of the 23.2 percent total. Third,
blacks (women only) made only modest progress in terms of movement into high income employment (from zero to 3.4 percent),
while white women moved from zero to 27.6 percent. Unlike the
middle sector, high income mobility for white women occurred
wholly in the 1970-75 period.

In sum, by the end of the decade, white males had lost
their position of complete dominance in the high and middle
income sectors. In the middle sector this loss results in
rough proportional representation for blacks and women, however, in the high income sector white males, approximately 12
percent of the industry, continue to dominate with a 69 percent
share.

Boston

In Table 5.6 data on ethno-sex mobility in the Boston
health industry are reported. The first thing to note is that
in the high income sector blacks, approximately 6 percent of
the industry, are not represented in 1965, 1970 or 1975. In
the middle sector, blacks in 1965 held a 4.6 percent share divided equally between men and women but by 1970 this share declines to 2.5 percent, .8 percent for men and 1.7 percent for
women. Between 1970-75 there is a dramatic increase, from 2.5
percent to 7.7 percent with most of the increase occurring for
women (1.7 percent to 5.5 percent compared to .8 percent to
1.9 percent for men). This 7.7 percent share exceeds the black
proportion in the industry for males and females and, unlike
Houston, blacks in Boston are not disproportionately represented in the low income sector. Indeed, in 1975 the black share
of low income jobs was less than their total industry share.
Also, it should be noted that in Boston, again unlike Houston,
blacks in 1965 held a reasonable share of middle sector jobs.
Finally, the period 1965-70 was one of decline while 1970-75
was one of growth.

TABLE 5.6

ETHNO-SEX MOBILITY, HEALTH, BOSTON,

1965, 1970, 1975

	1965			1970			1975		
	Low	Mid	High	Low	Mid	High	Low	Mid	High
Blacks	6.8%	4.6%	0	9.7%	2.5%	0	5.6%	7.7%	0
Males	1.5%	2.3%	0	2.1%	.8%	0	1.9%	1.9%	0
Females	5.3%	2.3%	0	7.6%	1.7%	0	3.7%	5.8%	0
Whites	93.2%	95.4%	100%	90.3%	97.5%	100%	94.4%	92.3%	100%
Males	16.5%	41.9%	83.7%	15.8%	20.8%	95.8%	16.1%	20.7%	68.8%
Females	76.7%	53.5%	16.3%	74.5%	76.7%	4.2%	78.3%	71.6%	31.2%

Turning to white females, the period began and ended with
approximate proportional representation in the low income segment and in the middle income segment women, slightly more than
70 percent of the industry, held a 53.5 percent share in 1965,
by 1970 this increases to 76.7 percent and then declines to
71.6 percent by 1975. Thus the period 1965-70 represents one
of considerable middle sector mobility for white women (the
share held by white men declines from 41.9 percent to 20.7
percent) and the period 1970-75 represents one of modest decline.

In the high income sector, one observes a curious pattern
with respect to time. In 1965 white women held a 16.3 percent
share of the higher paying jobs but by 1970 this declines to
4.2 percent (we should recall that blacks too lost shares during this period but with respect to middle sector employment).
But between 1970-75, there is a dramatic change, from 4.2 percent to 31.2 percent in the five years. Thus, overall the
share of high income jobs held by white males declines from
83.7 percent to 68.8 percent, compared to their approximately
22 percent of the industry.

The following patterns, then, are revealed for Boston.
First, with respect to blacks we observe throughout the period
no representation in the higher paying jobs. In the middle
sector, the black share declines in the period 1965-70, but
increases to above parity in the period 1970-75. While blacks
are not represented in the high income sector, they are not
disproportionately represented in lowest paying sector either.
For white women the period 1965-70 was also retrogressive but
in the high rather than middle sector. They lost high income
shares to white men in 1965-70 but made significant progress
between 1970-75. In the middle sector, white females achieve
more than parity between 1965-70 and then decline between
1970-75 to approximate parity. Thus, we find complete white
dominance of high income jobs, parity for blacks in the middle
sector, parity for women in the middle sector but in spite of
some mobility for white women, white male dominance of high
paying jobs.

Electronics

U.S.A.

Table 5.7 presents the data on ethno-sex mobility in the
electrical manufacturing industry in the United States. Examining blacks first, in 1965 they constituted 5.4 percent of
the industry, in 1970 7.7 percent and in 1975 8.4 percent
(throughout males constituted approximately two-thirds of this
number). Steady growth is observed in all income categories
during the ten years with no significant differences with re-

TABLE 5.7

ETHNO-SEX MOBILITY, ELECTRICAL MANUFACTURING, U.S.A.,

1965, 1970, 1975

	1965			1970			1975		
	Low	Mid	High	Low	Mid	High	Low	Mid	High
Blacks	6.9%	4.2%	.1%	11.9%	6.3%	.5%	13%	8.7%	3.1%
Males	4.9%	4.0%	.1%	6.8%	5.5%	.5%	6.9%	6.6%	3%
Females	2%	.2%	0	4.9%	.8%	0	6.1%	2.1%	.1%
Whites	93.2%	95.8%	99.9%	88.3%	93.7%	99.5%	86.9%	91.2%	96.9%
Males	56.6%	91.2%	99.0%	42.6%	82.4%	98.5%	44.7%	69%	94.1%
Females	36.6%	4.6%	.9%	45.7%	11.3%	1%	42.2%	22.2%	2.8%

spect to time period. In the low income category, the black
share nearly doubled between 1965 and 1975, from 6.9 percent
to 13 percent, compared to their 8.4 percent share of total
industry employment. And the Table shows that by 1975 this
black share of low income employment is divided nearly equally
between males and females.

In the middle income sector, during the decade, blacks
achieve parity, from 4.2 percent in 1965 to 8.7 percent in
1975. The black male share exceeds parity by more than a
point and black females achieve near parity, 2.1 percent compared to 2.5 percent of the industry with most of the growth
occurring in the 1970-75 period.

In terms of the highest paying jobs, some mobility is observed for black males but hardly any for black females. In
1965 blacks held a bare .1 percent of high income employment,
all held by black men. Between 1965 and 1970 there was minimal
movement to .5 percent, again all held by males. But between
1970-75 there was more significant progress, from .5 percent
to 3.1 percent, all but .1 percent held by men. Thus by the
end of the decade black men had achieved somewhat more than a
third of their share of high income employment. Black women
with no representation in 1965 during the decade made essentially no progress, ending in 1975 with .1 percent.

Turning to whites, in 1965 males dominated the middle and
high income categories while white women, approximately 20
percent of the labor force, were concentrated in the low income sector, 36.6 percent in 1965, 45.7 percent in 1970 and
42.2 percent in 1975. Some mobility is observed for women at
the middle level, increasing from 4.6 percent to 11.3 percent
in 1970 and to 22.2 percent in 1975, which corresponds to
their representation in the industry as a whole. In the high
income category, women made relatively little progress, from
.9 percent in 1965 to 2.8 percent by 1975. As in the case of
middle sector mobility, progress here is most pronounced in
the 1970-75 period.

Thus by the end of the decade white women remained disproportionately represented in the low income category, achieved
parity in the middle sector and remained underrepresented in
the highest paying jobs; white males, about 70 percent of the
labor force, held 94.1 percent of best paying jobs.

Houston

The data on ethno-sex mobility in the electrical manufacturing industry of Houston reported in Table 5.8 show that in
1965 the industry, except for the low income segment, was dominated by whites. Black women were not represented in the industry in 1965 and the 7.1 percent share held by black men were
nearly all employed in the low income segment, none in the

TABLE 5.8

ETHNO-SEX MOBILITY, ELECTRICAL MANUFACTURING, HOUSTON, 1965, 1970, 1975

	1965			1970			1975		
	Low	Mid	High	Low	Mid	High	Low	Mid	High
Blacks	14.5%	.8%	0	20.7%	10.4%	4.4%	17.3%	13.5%	7.9%
Males	14.5%	0	0	14.9%	10.4%	4.4%	9.3%	13.1%	7.9%
Females	0	0	0	8%	0	0	8%	.4%	0
Whites	85.5%	99.2%	100%	79.3%	89.6%	95.6%	82.7%	86.5%	92.1%
Males	70%	91.9%	100%	57%	79.7%	92.6%	52%	69.7%	90.1%
Females	15.5%	7.3%	0	22.3%	9.7%	3%	30.7%	16.8%	2%

high income category and a miniscule .8 percent in the middle. In the ten years black males made significant progress at the middle level, especially in the period 1965-70, exceeding parity by 1975 (11.2 percent industry share compared to a 13.1 percent middle sector share). During this period mobility for black males is also observed in the high income category, from 0 to 4.4 percent between 1965-70 and by 1975 by 7.9 percent, roughly two-thirds parity.

Black women enter the industry in 1970 with a 1.7 percent share, all in the low income category. By 1975 this remains virtually unchanged at 1.6 percent with all save .4 percent in the low income segment. Thus we observe little mobility for black women largely because they have barely penetrated the industry.

Between 1965 and 1975 white males maintained their dominance in the high income sector while white women made some progress at the middle level. In 1965 white males, approximately 80 percent of the industry, held 100 percent of the highest paying jobs, in 1970 the numbers were 75 percent and 92.6 percent respectively and in 1975 71 percent and 90 percent. Thus white females were barely able to penetrate the high income segment. Ranging from 12-15 percent of the industry during the decade, in 1965 they held none of the best paying jobs, in 1970 three percent, but by 1975 it was down to two percent.

In the middle sector, we observe a greater degree of mobility for white women. In 1965 women held a 7.3 percent share, in 1970 9.9 percent and in 1975 16.8 percent, which is somewhat above their proportion of the industry work force. Conversely, male shares in this sector decline from 91.9 percent in 1965 to a proportional 69.7 percent by 1975.

Thus by the end of the decade, white women were disproportionately represented in the low income sector, proportionally represented in the middle sector and substantially underrepresented in the high income segment. The 1970-75 period is the most productive in terms of middle sector mobility, while it is a period of decline insofar as high income mobility is concerned.

Boston

The data are reported in Table 5.9 on the ethno-sex distribution of persons in the electrical manufacturing industry of Boston. The data are consistent with that observed in the nation and Houston in terms of the mobility of blacks and women. We find dominance by white males in the high income sector, rough parity for blacks and women in the middle sector and disproportionate representation of blacks but especially women in the low income sector.

TABLE 5.9

ETHNO-SEX MOBILITY, ELECTRICAL MANUFACTURING INDUSTRY, BOSTON,

1965, 1970, 1975

	1965			1970			1975		
	Low	Mid	High	Low	Mid	High	Low	Mid	High
Blacks	3.4%	1.3%	0	5.6%	2.1%	0	5.9%	4.5%	1.9%
Males	1.3%	.9%	0	2.6%	1.5%	0	3.5%	2.6%	1.6%
Females	2.1%	.4%	0	3%	.6%	0	2.4%	1.9%	.3%
Whites	96.6%	98.7%	100%	94.4%	97.9%	100%	94.1%	95.5%	98.1%
Males	47.6%	94%	100%	35.5%	85.2%	98.5%	35.5%	60.7%	95.7%
Females	49%	4.7%	0	58.9%	12.7%	1.5%	58.6%	34.8%	2.4%

    With respect to blacks, ranging from 2.5 percent in 1965
to 4.1 percent in 1975 of the industry labor, they constituted
3.4 percent of the low income segment in 1965, 5.6 percent in
1970 and 5.9 percent in 1975. Thus throughout the ten years
there was some degree of concentration of blacks, male and female, in the low paying sector of the industry. In the middle
income sector, we observe an increasing share for blacks during
the decade, from 1.3 percent in 1965 to 4.5 percent in 1975.
Most of the increase occurred in the period 1970-75 and it was
shared equally by males and females such that by 1975 black
men and women had achieved proportional representation in the
middle income segment.
    In the high income category, some mobility is observed but
not enough to achieve proportional representation. In 1965
and 1970 no black representation in this category is observed
but by 1975 they achieve a 1.9 percent share, a little less
than half their proportion of the industry as a whole. Black
men with a 1.6 percent share did considerably better than
black women with a mere .3 percent share.
    Turning to white females, approximately 30 percent of the
labor force, in 1965 they constituted 49 percent of the low income segment, 4.7 percent of the middle and they were not represented in the high income category. By 1970 the figures were
58.9 percent low income, 12.7 percent middle and 1.5 percent
high and by 1975 they were 58.6 percent, 34.8 percent and 2.4
percent respectively. Thus, at the end of the ten year period
white women were even more concentrated in the low income category (58.6 percent low income compared to 31.6 percent of total
industry employment), achieve rough parity in the middle sector
but remain substantially underrepresented in the high income
sector; white males, approximately 64 percent of the industry,
begin and end the ten year period with more than 95 percent of
high income employment.
    In Boston, then, the following patterns are observed.
First, concentration of blacks but especially women in the low
income category, considerable mobility for blacks and women at
the middle level such that parity is achieved by 1975 and continued dominance by white males of high income employment although during the decade blacks achieve roughly half parity
while women remain substantially underrepresented. Finally for
both blacks and women 1970-75 rather than 1965-70 shows more
rapid growth.

The Impact of EEOC

    In order to more sensitively assess black and female occu-
pational mobility (through analysis of occupational in addition
to wage categories) in the two industries and to make some inferences about the impact of EEOC activity (as a surrogate for

government anti-discrimination activity) we obtained unpublished EEOC EEO-1 reports for the Houston and Boston SMSAs
for the years 1966, 1970 and 1976.1

Beginning first with the probable impact of EEOC activity
on black and female access to employment, we first sought to
get a measure of such activity. We obtained from the Commission a list of cases filed between 1972 and 1978 (the Commission did not possess litigation authority until 1972) in the
Federal District Court of Massachusetts and the Southern District of Texas (covering Houston). The Commission filed
eighteen civil actions regarding employment discrimination in
Massachusetts and thirty-three in the Southern District of
Texas, an indicator of somewhat more government anti-discrimination activity in Houston than Boston.

An inspection of the lists of cases shows that in Houston
five cases (15 percent) were brought against electrical manufacturing firms and none against institutions or firms in the
health industry. In Boston one case (6 percent) was filed
against a hospital and three (17 percent) against firms and a
union local in the electrical manufacturing industry. Thus
while there was more EEOC litigation in the federal court jur-
isdiction in Houston than in Boston, in terms of our specific
industries we find slightly more targeted activity in Boston.

Examining the penetration of blacks and women in the
electrical manufacturing and health industries of Houston and
Boston, in Tables 5.10 and 5.11 data on percent distribution
for those firms covered by EEOC under Title VII of the Civil
Rights Act of 1964 compared to the CWHS data (which include
employees in firms not covered by EEOC) for the years 1966,
1970 and 1975.

The data show that in general blacks during the ten year
period make more progress in penetrating firms covered by EEOC
in both Houston and Boston then they do in industry generally
as covered by CWHS. For white females the opposite is the
case; they show more penetration in both cities and industries
in firms generally as reported in the CWHS data than they do
in those firms reporting to the EEOC. Although the data reported here are too crude to be anything more than suggestive,
the suggestion is that government anti-discrimination activity
is more effective in raising the labor market status of blacks
than white women. Although there was more activity in Houston
than Boston but more industry specific activity in the latter,
the data does not suggest a differential impact of EEOC activity in Houston and Boston as an explanatory factor in black
penetration of the two industries.

The EEOC data also permit the more refined analysis of
black and female mobility because using it we can examine progress through occupational categories as well as wage hierarchies. The EEOC data show that in the health industry white
women in both Houston and Boston are proportionally represented

TABLE 5.10

COMPARISON OF EEOC AND CWHS PENETRATION (IN PERCENT) OF BLACKS AND WHITE
FEMALES IN THE HEALTH INDUSTRY, HOUSTON AND BOSTON, 1965, 1970, 1975*

HOUSTON

	1966				1970				1975			
	Blacks	Black Males	Black Females	White Females	Blacks	Black Males	Black Females	White Females	Blacks	Black Males	Black Females	White Females
CWHS	22.9	5.8	17.1	63.1	26.6	2.6	24	59.6	28.1	3.2	24.9	59.9
EEOC	30	8	22	48	32	6	26	47	34	5	29	46

BOSTON

	1966				1970				1975			
	Blacks	Black Males	Black Females	White Females	Blacks	Black Males	Black Females	White Females	Blacks	Black Males	Black Females	White Females
CWHS	6.6	1.5	5.1	74.4	7.4	1.7	5.7	73.2	6.2	1.8	4.4	71.9
EEOC	7	2	5	69	7	2	5	68	8	2	6	66

*EEOC data are for 1966, CWHS data are for 1965.

TABLE 5.11

COMPARISON OF EEOC AND CWHS PENETRATION (PERCENT) OF BLACKS AND WHITE

FEMALES IN THE ELECTRICAL MANUFACTURING INDUSTRY,

HOUSTON AND BOSTON, 1966, 1970, 1975*

HOUSTON

	1966				1970				1975			
	Blacks	Black Males	Black Females	White Females	Blacks	Black Males	Black Females	White Females	Blacks	Black Males	Black Females	White Females
CWHS	7.1	7.1	0	10.7	12.4	10.7	1.7	12.4	12.8	11.2	1.6	15.8
EEOC	7	7	0	11	12	10	2	14	16	12	4	13

BOSTON

	1966				1970				1975			
	Blacks	Black Males	Black Females	White Females	Blacks	Black Males	Black Females	White Females	Blacks	Black Males	Black Females	White Females
CWHS	2.5	1.1	1.4	30.1	3.1	1.7	1.4	28.3	4.1	2.5	1.6	31.6
EEOC	2	1	1	29	3	2	1	27	4	3	1	25

*EEOC data are for 1966, CWHS data are for 1965.

in all job categories (professional-technical, clerical, craft, operative-laborer) except sales, where white males are dominant. In Boston, white females, approximately 70 percent of the industry, decline from a 23 percent share in the sales category to 15 percent between 1966 and 1970 and then increase to 35 percent by 1975. And in Houston their share of sales employment decreases from 12 to 10 percent between 1966 and 1970 and then rises to 25 percent by 1975, still considerably below their two-thirds share of industry employment as a whole.

Blacks in the Houston and Boston health industry are underrepresented in professional-technical categories, somewhat overrepresented in the operative-laborer categories and approach parity in the other categories. In Houston, however, black women have a larger share of employment in the sales category than they do in Boston.

In the electrical manufacturing industry of Boston white women are concentrated in clerical and operative and while some modest progress is observed in the professional-technical categories (3 percent - 8 percent) and sales (5 percent - 6 percent) between 1966 and 1975, it is not enough to alter the pattern of under-utilization in these job categories. Black males in Boston achieve parity in the sales categories, roughly half parity in professional-operative-laborer categories. Black women are found only in the clerical and operative categories with little representation in sales or professional-technical.[2]

In general, then, analysis of the occupation specific data from the EEOC regarding black and female mobility is not inconsistent with the findings from the analysis of the CWHS wage data, except that in Boston blacks are concentrated in the low wage occupations, but a similar disparate affect is not observed in the wage data. In addition, in the health industry women have achieved proportionate representation in professional-technical categories yet probably because of their tendency to be nurses rather than physicians their occupational success does not translate into wages commensurate with those of white males.

Summary

Unlike the pattern reported in Chapter 4 with respect to penetration, geographic locale and industry do not appear to make a difference insofar as mobility is concerned. Rather, the patterns are basically the same in Houston, Boston and the nation and in other industries, health and electrical manufacturing. Essentially the patterns are white male dominance in the high income employment category, the achievement in the period 1965-75 of proportionate representation in middle income category by both blacks and women and the disproportionate representation of blacks and women in low income employment sector.   While there are variations (black women, for example, appear to do better in health in Houston than in Boston or the nation), fundamentally the cities and industries are more similar than not with respect to black and female mobility.   Thus, the basic conclusion to be drawn from the analysis of the data on mobility is that factors explaining the access of disadvantaged groups to employment are not the same as those that explain mobility.

It appears that mobility is to a considerable extent a function of initial penetration.   That is, the data show that once blacks and white women achieve a given level of representation in an industry, progress through wage categories is steady and consistent across cities and industries until within a decade parity is achieved in the middle income sector.   This suggests that for both white females and blacks mobility in U.S. industry occurs more as a result of within industry promotions than it does as a result of initial penetration at the higher paying levels.   This also suggests that in the next decade or so progress should be observed for blacks and white women in the upper income categories but of course this is dependent on continued initial penetration and continued mobility at the middle income level.

NOTES

1.   The Employer Information Reports, EEO-1, are the only source of current comprehensive statistical information on the employment of minorities and women in private industry, by occupational category for the United States and its subdivisions.   The EEO-1 provides employment statistics by sex, for each of nine major occupational groups and for each of four minority groups: blacks, Hispanics, Asian-Americans and American Indians.

2.   In Houston, Hispanics decline from eight percent to seven percent of the health labor force between 1966 and 1975 while in Boston they increase from one percent to two percent.   In Houston they achieve proportional representation in all job categories by 1975 but in Boston they are concentrated in the operative-laborer categories.   In the electrical manufacturing industry, Hispanics in Houston increase their share of employment from 4 percent in 1966 to 13 percent in 1975 and in Boston from .4 percent to 2 percent.   In both cities Hispanic workers tend to be disproportionately represented in the operative-laborer categories and underrepresented in the professional-technical categories, however, more apparent mobility is observed in Houston than Boston.

CHAPTER 6
Summary and Conclusion

This study of two industries in two local labor markets was undertaken to provide some tentative answers to questions regarding the impact of geographic place, time, industry and group characteristics on employment opportunities for blacks and women in the United States. In particular, we were interested in investigating, at least preliminarily, the impact of the differential patterns of employment growth in "snowbelt" and "sunbelt" on the prospects for the employment and mobility of groups historically disadvantaged in the labor market.

Analysis of the data on penetration and mobility in the health and electrical manufacturing industries compared with all other industry in Houston, Boston and the nation suggests six fundamental conclusions. First, growth in the economy is not the fundamental determinant of black and female employment opportunities. Second, what are usually called non-economic variables, that is local political cultures and structures, may operate as intervening variables to structure the operations of local labor markets in terms of black and female access. Third, industries differ in the extent to which they provide employment opportunities for blacks and women. Fourth, while there are differences by city and industry regarding the penetration of women and blacks, insofar as mobility is concerned the patterns are basically the same regardless of industry and place. Fifth, there are differences with respect to time in the employment and mobility of blacks and women. Finally, government anti-discrimination activity varies by industry in its affect and it has a differential impact on the employment opportunities of blacks and women.

In this chapter, we explicate the foregoing concluding points, discuss the impact of group characteristics in terms of educational attainments, draw important methodological outcomes of the study, suggest directions for further research

85

and discuss some of the policy implications that may be
gleaned from the research.

Basic Conclusions

The most basic difference between the Houston and Boston
labor markets is in terms of economic growth. In Boston, between 1960 and 1974 growth in employment is estimated at 19
percent while in Houston in this period it is estimated at 106
percent. And in the most recent period, 1975-79, manufacturing
employment in Houston grew by 20.5 percent and in Boston by 7.5
percent. And the official unemployment rate in Houston during
this period hovered near or above what some economists call
full employment (4 percent or less) while the Boston rate was
near twice that. In mid 1980, for example, BLS data show an
unemployment rate of 3.1 percent in Houston, and 5 percent in
Boston.
The general pattern of economic growth in the two cities
is reflected in their respective health and electrical manufacturing industries. In Houston, employment in the health industry between 1970-75 grew by 47 percent and in the electrical
manufacturing industry by 138 percent, while in Boston the respective numbers are 27 percent and 24 percent. Thus in terms
of the presumptive determinative impact of growth and tight
labor markets on the employment opportunities of historically
disadvantaged groups, Houston and Boston are critical case
studies. And the data are unequivocal: blacks and women do not
find substantially more employment opportunities (in terms of
penetration or mobility) in the rapidly growing Houston labor
market than they do in the slower growing Boston labor market.
Given the magnitude of the growth differentials between
the two cities, if employment growth is fundamentally determinative of black and female access to employment opportunities
then differences would surely emerge in our data. But, in
fact, the differences are minor and indeed except for black wom-
en in Houston's health industry the marginal differences suggest that blacks find somewhat more employment opportunity in
terms of penetration in Boston than they do in Houston.
This study then joins that body of literature that suggests employment growth per se is not the predominant factor
in explaining the growth of minority employment.[1] This finding has important implications in the development of macro
and micro economic policy and the development of effective
equal employment policies. We discuss these implications below, but first the fact that Boston's labor market appears
marginally more conducive to black employment opportunities
argues that Hiestand and others are correct in their conclusion that non-economic variables, particularly the political
and social environment, are more important in changing the

economic position of minorities, especially blacks, than economic specific variables.

In regard to these non-economic variables, Houston and
Boston are again critical cases. We presented evidence in
Chapter 2 to show that Houston and Boston differ significantly
in terms of political culture, to some extent in terms of political structure and substantially in terms of race ethos.
Stated succinctly, the evidence presented shows that Boston,
notwithstanding the racial tensions revealed by the desegregation of the schools, is a more liberal, racially progressive
city than Houston. And studies have shown that the political
environment or culture, especially the general attitude toward
blacks in the community, are more important than economic specific variables in shaping black access to employment.[2] Thus
this study provides modest support for the emergent proposition
in the economics of discrimination literature regarding the importance of political and social variables in explaining black
access to employment opportunities.

As anticipated the data show that blacks but especially
women find more employment opportunities in the health industry
than in other industry generally or in the electrical manufacturing industry. But there is some evidence that blacks, especially males, are losing shares of employment in the industry.
In Boston and the nation the black share of total health industry employment declined between 1970 and 1975. In the nation
the shares were lost basically by black males with consequent
gains by white males and females alike while in Boston the shares
were lost basically by black women to white men. In Houston,
on the other hand, the black share increases substantially but
only black women share in the increase as the proportion of employment in the Houston health industry held by black men declines between 1965-75. Thus the data in this study to some
extent support the National Commission for Manpower's 1976 warning that as wages and working conditions in the industry improve disadvantaged workers may begin to lose their traditional
positions as favored employees.[3] This was at least the case
insofar as black workers are concerned.

Women, black and white, find more employment opportunity
in other industry underrepresented while black men do as well
or better in electrical manufacturing as in other industry in
all places--Houston, Boston and the nation. Thus, we conclude
that regarding equal employment opportunity in the United
States industry specific considerations are important.

While industry and geographic locale are important determinants of black and female employment, they are not central in
patterns of mobility. The pattern, white male dominance in the
high income employment category, the achievement in the period
1965-75 of proportionate or near proportionate representation
in the middle income category and the disproportionate representation of blacks and women in the low income sector, is

basically the same in Houston, Boston and the nation and in other industry, health and electrical manufacturing. Thus another basic conclusion - one with important policy import - is that patterns of employment differ from patterns of mobility.

Because of the presumed impact of the Civil Rights Act of 1964 and consequent heightened anti-discrimination activity by the government, because the mid 1960s was a period of sustained economic growth and because the late 1960s and early 1970s was a period of slow economic growth and less intensive government anti-discrimination activity, we decided to partition our study into the periods 1965-70 and 1970-75 in order to glean some insights into the dynamics of these factors.

Although there is variation (growth and decline for some groups in some industries and locales in both time periods), generally, as might have been anticipated, the 1965-70 period is the most productive in terms of penetration while 1970-75 appears most productive in terms of mobility. Again, the pattern of penetration in 1965-70, mobility in 1970-75 to some extent is to be expected since some proportion of the observed mobility is probably a function of promotions and one has to be in a job before one can be promoted. A significant finding here also is that in spite of the most severe recession since the depression, one does not observe significant relative changes in employment and mobility of blacks and women.

Finally, regarding the affect of government anti-discrimination activity, in Chapter 2 we reported data that indicated little EEOC impact on black and female mobility in private industry in Houston and Boston. However, data reported in Chapter 5 on penetration in the health and electrical manufacturing industries of the two cities does suggest an impact insofar as blacks are concerned. Specifically, the data show that in general blacks during the ten year period made more progress in penetrating EEOC covered firms in Houston and Boston than non-EEOC covered firms while white females made more progress in non-EEOC covered firms in the two cities than in EEOC covered firms.

In general, then, the admittedly limited data of this study suggests that the impact of government anti-discrimination activity varies by industry; that government anti-discrimination activity is more effective in terms of penetration than it is in terms of mobility and that government anti-discrimination activity is more effective in raising the labor market status of blacks than white women.[4]

The Impact of the Educational Gap

Ideally, as Friedlander points out, the educational gap should be measured by quality of job vacancies against quality of unemployed labor, plus potential labor force entrants.[5]

However, data limitations require use of formal educational attainments as a surrogate measure of employee qualifications.

Using this measure, there is not a significant educational gap between males and females in Houston or Boston. In the
former, the median years of education for males is 12.1, for
females 12 and in the latter the median years of education is
12.4 for both males and females. We infer from these data
that the male-female employment and mobility differential observed in the industries of Houston and Boston is probably not
a function to any significant degree of a gap in educational
attainment.

The case of blacks is different.   There is a significant
educational gap between blacks and whites in the two cities.
In Houston median years of education for black males is 10 compared to 12.1 for white males and for women the respective figures are 10.6 and 12. And in Boston median years of education
for black males is 11.6 compared to 12.4 for white males and
11.7 for black females compared to 12.4 for white females.

In addition to this statistical gap, studies have shown
that comparing black and white students with the "same amount"
of education may be misleading since black students (and others from disadvantaged backgrounds) tend not to "know" as much
(as measured by performance on standard assessment examina-
tions in mathematics, science and English) as their white
counterparts.[6]

The strong implication of these data, then, is that the
observed black-white differential in employment and mobility in
Houston and Boston may be to some extent explained by the educational gap. This inference is further supported when it is
recalled that blacks do marginally better in terms of employment in Boston where the educational gap is smaller than they
do in Houston where it is somewhat larger.

However, we should be careful in drawing this inference
since there is a growing body of literature that suggests that
employers use educational attainments as a screening device
to eliminate applicants rather than to choose the most qualified.   That is, they tend to be relatively unconcerned about
the content of education but regard the diploma or degree as
a rough index of capability and reliability.[7] Consequently,
there has emerged in recent years what might be called "credential inflation" whereby more and more people are required to
complete more and more education to qualify for jobs where the
education is not needed.[8] Clearly, such inflation in credentials works to the disadvantage of blacks and other insular
minorities especially in the health industry where inflation
in credentials is widespread. Goldstein and Horowitz report
in 1974 no less than 540 specialty groups, other than physicians in the health industry and they argue that this special-
ization prevents the optimal utilization of health personnel
and operate as a barrier to job opportunities for the poor,

the disadvantaged and those with little education.[9]

Thus, while there is a black-white education gap, one should be careful in drawing inferences about its relationship to employee qualifications. Finally, whatever the relationship between educational attainment and employee qualification Friedlander after study of minority rates of unemployment in thirty cities writes "... the cautious conclusion is that education per se, and even the educational gap, are not so important as we had expected in explaining the differences among these cities in the rates of unemployment."[10] While factors explaining minority unemployment are not necessarily the same as those explaining the employment and mobility of minorities, Friedlander's conclusion regarding the role of the education gap is important because it suggests that one should be cautious in positing relationships between education and access to employment opportunities.

Methodological Outcome

This study sought to demonstrate the value of a micro level approach to studies in employment discrimination as a supplement to the typical macro work in the field. Despite the paucity of data at the level of city and industry, it is appropriate to attempt to identify in some detail distinctive features of particular industries in particular locales that play a significant part in the employment and mobility of black and female workers. We were searching for the common and distinctive characteristics underlying micro level labor market dynamics with an eye toward proposing consideration of these local dimensions in such a way as to construct sensitive and responsive national equal employment policies. While this work is preliminary in character, tentative rather than definitive, it does, we believe, suggest the utility of research that focuses on local labor markets and industries in an effort to identify factors that facilitate the provision of jobs and career opportunities to disadvantaged groups.[11]

The study also demonstrates the usefulness of the Social Security data in research of this kind. The CWHS is a micro data file in that it contains information on individual workers. Thus inferences can be made about the processes through which economic and demographic changes take place in particular areas and industries. Although the CWHS data cover fewer persons (the working population with social security covered jobs rather than total population) and fewer demographic characteristics than census data, we believe our work shows that its unique capability to provide year-by-year data on the same workers outweighs its limitations in coverage.[12]

We of course have not fully exploited the potential of the CWHS data in this report. In terms of directions for fur-

ther research, the data in the sample are reported for labor
force members by their place of work rather than their place
of residence, thus it is possible to trace occupational migration as well as penetration and mobility. This can be done by
noting for each year in a measuring period and for each city
and industry the number of each race-sex group that (a) held
jobs in that occupation in that city in the previous year;
(b) held jobs in another occupational category but worked in
that city the previous year; (c) held jobs in that occupation
but not in that city the previous year; and (d) are not record-
ed as holding a job the previous year. This approach would
permit the exact specification of the migration process of individuals from occupations, industries and cities. This would
be particularly useful in detailing exactly who it is that is
benefiting from the rapid increase in employment in sunbelt
cities.

Further work should also include a larger sample of cities (to, for example, study the impact of black mayors on minority employment and mobility in local labor markets) and industries (including a declining one such as steel). Broadly,
comparative research of this character would facilitate the
more rigorous quantification of the impact of social, cultural,
political and economic-specific variables as they impact on
the employment opportunities of disadvantaged groups. Finally,
future research should probably include interviews with local
labor market, political, interest groups and equal employment
officials to improve our understanding beyond that provided by
the statistical data.

Implications

This study joins that body of research on employment discrimination that concludes that growth per se is not the key
determinant of equal employment opportunity but rather it suggests that structural differences between cities in terms of
economic base, political culture and patterns of institutional
racism are also important variables. In terms of policy, this
study then challenges the easy assumptions of the "growth
school" that mere increases an aggregate demand is sufficient
to remedy problems of the effects of racism and sexism in the
labor market.[13]
This has an important implication for policy makers in an
era when the economy is not expected to grow fast enough to
insure full employment[14] and where the growth that is project-
ed is expected to be most rapid and sustained in that part of
the country where race and perhaps sex privilege in the labor
market has been most historic and pervasive.[15] Thus, we would
suggest that positive state action is probably a necessary ac-
companiment of any public policy that is to be effective in

assuring equal employment opportunity in the United States. That is, in order to further improve the labor market status of the disadvantaged one cannot rely on a rapidly growing economy alone.

The differences in economic base, political culture and social structure between Houston and Boston (and probably snowbelt and sunbelt cities generally) counsel against designing manpower and equal employment policies for one city in the same way as one would design them for the other. That is, it is necessary to take account of local variations in labor markets and variations in political culture and structure. For it is likely that black and female employment opportunities are to some extent shaped more by these local factors than they are by national level changes in the economy. Indeed, a major assumption of the present study is that more attention should be paid to the specifics of local labor markets and political systems in the design and implementation of employment and manpower policies. For example, it may very well be that black employment opportunities are a function of black political power, thus to increase the latter is to increase the former. Other examples could be cited; the point is that national policy makers should be sensitive to these kinds of variations and relationships in the design of effective national manpower and equal opportunity policies.

Finally, in the enforcement of the government's varied anti-discrimination policies this study suggests that policy makers should focus their attention at the hierarchy of the wage and occupational structure of United States industry. This is so because in all places and in all industries we find that blacks and women have achieved parity or near parity in the middle income category during the ten year period, 1965-75. However, in all places and industries they remain underrepresented in the high wage sector where white males between 1964-75 maintained their dominant position. The evidence indicates that this underrepresentation in the high wage sector may be a function of length of time in the industry. To the extent this is the case, considerable upper income mobility should be observed in all places and industries for blacks and women in the next decade. However, length of time in the industry notwithstanding, it is at the upper income level that the equal employment opportunity bureaucracies of government ought to focus their resources.

Yet, as Butler and Heckman point out, having too many blacks in low skilled occupations is just as much a violation of the principle of affirmative action as having too few blacks in high skilled occupations.[16] In Boston the data does not show substantial evidence of disproportionate representation of blacks in low income employment, but in Houston and in the nation there is such evidence and thus equal employment policy in these places should focus on both the top and bottom of the wage structure. What must be shown is that the concentration of blacks or women in the low wage sector is a result of a skill-education gap in the same way as it must be shown that their underrepresentation in the high wage category is also a function of the lack of labor market availability of qualified blacks and women.

NOTES

1. See for example Dale L. Hiestand, Economic Growth and Employment Opportunities for Minorities (New York: Columbia University Press, 1964) and Stanley L. Friedlander, Unemployment in the Urban Core: An Analysis of Thirty Cities with Policy Recommendations (New York: Praeger, 1972).
2. Barbara Bergmann and Jerolyn Lyle, "Differences Among Metropolitan Areas and Industries in the Occupational Standing of Negroes in the Private Sector" (College Park, Maryland: Project on the Economics of Discrimination, 1970). See also Ray Marshall, "The Economics of Racial Discrimination: A Survey," Journal of Economic Literature (September 1978), pp. 849-71.
3. Employment Impact of Health Policy Developments, Special Report No. 11 (Washington, D.C.: National Commission for Manpower Policy, 1976), p. 20.
4. There is considerable dispute among specialists as to the affect of government anti-discrimination policy on black employment and mobility. For a review of the literature see Richard Butler and James Heckman, "The Government's Impact on the Labor Market Status of Blacks: A Critical Review" (Chicago: Industrial Relations Association Series, Equal Rights and Industrial Relations, 1977).
5. Friedlander, Unemployment in the Urban Core, p. 61.
6. See the data cited in Chapter 2 from the National Assessment of Educational Progress and John Ogbu, Minority Education and Caste (New York: Academic Press, 1978), Chaps. 2 and 3.
7. Ogbu, Minority Education and Caste, Chaps. 5-6.
8. Randall Collings presents a thoughtful and in some ways brilliant historical and theoretical analysis of this phenomenon in his The Credential Society: An Historical Sociology of Education and Stratification (New York: Academic Press, 1979).
9. Harold M. Goldstein and Morris A. Horowitz, Health Personnel: Meeting the Explosive Demand for Health Care (Germantown, Md.: Aspen Systems Corporation, 1977).
10. Friedlander, Unemployment in the Urban Core, p. 69.
11. As a theoretical principle we would suggest that black employment opportunity like black political opportunity may be a function of varying local bases of institutional ra-

cism. The political scientist Hanes Walton, Jr. writes "... black politics is a function of the particular brand of segregation found in different environments in which black people find themselves. And the politics of blacks differ significantly from locality to locality. Although there are many striking similarities between the political activities of black Americans in different localities, there are differences far greater than geography can explain." See Black Politics: A Theoretical And Structural Analysis (New York: J. B. Lippincott, 1972).

12.   The limitations of the 1% sample have been substantially reduced by the development of a 10% sample. With inter-agency sponsorship from HUD and others, the Bureau of Economic Analysis and the Social Security Administration have developed data on migration and work force characteristics from 10% CWHS files for the first Quarters of 1971 and 1973 and work is underway to establish a 10% sample for the first Quarter of 1975.

13.   Stanley Greenberg, Race & State in Capitalist Development (New Haven: Yale University Press, 1980).

14.   Report of the National Commission on Technology, Automation and Economic Progress, Technology and the American Economy (Washington: Government Printing Office, 1966).

15.   George Sternlieb and James Hughes, Post Industrial America: Metropolitan Decline and Inter-Regional Job Shifts (New Brunswick, N.J.: Center for Urban Policy Research, 1976).

16.   Butler and Heckman, "The Government's Imapct on the Labor Market Status of Black Americans," p. 249.